THE HEART
OF THE CATSKILLS

Bob Steuding

PURPLE MOUNTAIN PRESS
Fleischmanns, New York

First Edition 2008

Published by Purple Mountain Press, Ltd.
P.O. Box 309, Fleischmanns, New York 12430-0309
845-254-4062, 845-254-4476 (fax), purple@catskill.net
http://www.catskill.net/purple

ISBN-13: 978-1-930098-92-3
ISBN: 1-930098-88-92-8
Library of Congress Control Number 2008935282

Cover: John Bill Rodgers (left) and Dick Misner.
Photo by Lionel De Lisser courtesy of Hope Farm Press.
Frontispiece: Peekamoose and Table Mountains, photo by the author.
Back cover: Author photo by Miles Steuding.

Illustrations, unless otherwise noted, are from the author's collection.

Manufactured in the United States of America on acid-free paper.

5 4 3 2 1

For Monica
My colleague and friend

"Whoever uses the local. . .
writes for numerous generations."

John Burroughs

CONTENTS

PREFACE

MORE THAN 30 YEARS AGO, while working on another book, I interviewed a woman, who, at the time, was over 100 years old. Her name was Mrs. Ferris Davis, and she was "sharp as a tack," as we say, and in full possession of her faculties. She had lived in the Esopus Valley before the construction of the Ashokan Reservoir, and was a descendant of the first people to settle there in the eighteenth century. But she was puzzled, wondering why I should wish to speak with her about her family. "We've lived, and that's all" she said, matter-of-factly. "It's a drawn-out story, and it doesn't amount to much." But I was deeply interested in that lost time and place. The study of the Catskill Mountains and those who have lived in them in the past, in fact, has become my lifework.

I can, also, remember talking with another woman named Jennie Kerr. She was 87 years old and the granddaughter of Catskill Mountain pioneers. When we spoke, many years ago, she was ill and would soon enter a nursing home, never to return to her beloved Catskills, again. Nonetheless, on a beautiful, clear, summer day, we drove up Watson Hollow near West Shokan, named for Nathan Watson, the man who operated the Metropolitan Tannery there in the nineteenth century and had cleared the neighboring mountains of all the hemlock. We ascended slowly the steep road, driving past the tannery site, now overgrown with hardwood. At the pass, called the "Gulf," where the road slices like a knife between Breath Hill and Little Rocky, my companion became excited, in anticipation of the return to the place of her youth. Near Peekamoose Lake, she pointed out Pencil Rock, where she and her classmates had gathered graphite, which they had used to write their lessons in school. She told me about the "Big Heads," a pioneer family who had settled in this area, now a part of the town of Denning. And this old woman, who had served as a practical nurse and had been the first person to drive a car in this part of the mountains, also informed me that the Picket Brook, above Peekamoose, a source of the Rondout Creek, had been settled by the Pickets in the early nineteenth century.

Beyond Peekamoose, we stopped beside the narrow, twisting mountain road and looked down at the "Blue Hole," a favorite swimming spot, cold and turquoise in the soft, filtered mountain light. We sat quietly together in the car for some time, saying nothing. Then, as if remembering the happy days of her childhood, days of hikes and blueberry picking, this woman, living out the last years of her long and full life, looked up towards the sheltering mountains above us and sadly said, "If only I could climb to the top of one of these mountains again. Oh, what I wouldn't give."

And so, I come, at last, to write this book. I have held on to these people and to this story for much too long. This place, and those who have settled it, their very names often forgotten, their lives marked only by a weathered gravestone or by the rubble of an abandoned farmhouse foundation found high up on the mountainside, have fascinated me since I was very young. If you find, while reading the pages which follow, that you have become captivated, as I have been charmed, by these people and by this place, then, I believe, I have, in some small measure, repaid the great debt which I feel— to this most interesting of regions, and to its inhabitants, who have shared with me the shape of their life and times.

BOB STEUDING
OLIVEBRIDGE, NEW YORK

The Southern Catskills

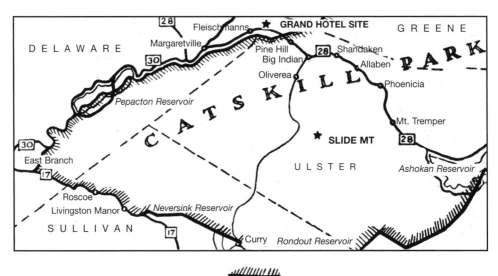

Catskill Park Boundry

CHAPTER 1
The Blue Mountains

U NTIL LATE into the nineteenth century, the Southern Catskills remained something of a mystery. For the most part, they were either misnamed or unknown. Although this area had been sparsely settled by the time of the American Revolution, and although, during the first half of the nineteenth century, the general depredation of the great forest, which covered this land like a vast, green tapestry had begun, in his massive study, *The Geography of New York*, state geographer J. H. Mather was to refer to the Southern Catskills in 1847 as simply "the Blue Mountains."[1] Even as late as 1853-1854, when the noted Hudson River School artist Asher B. Durand sketched and painted in the townships of Olive, Denning and Shandaken, he, too, incorrectly referred to this place as "the Shandaken Mountains."[2] Not until Professor Arnold Henry Guyot of Princeton University surveyed and mapped the Catskills in the 1860s and 1870s, dividing them into northern and southern sections, and proving that the lands to the southwest of the Esopus Creek were, in fact, part of the Catskill range, did interest shift from the Northern Catskills and the region of the Catskill Mountain House to these rugged and seemingly inhospitable mountains to the south.[3]

It was the naturalist John Burroughs, however, aided by extensive promotion initiated by the Ulster and Delaware Railroad, which began to serve this area in the early 1870s and opened the Grand Hotel above Pine Hill in 1881, who was to fix in the public mind this locale of wild lands, which stretch away from today's Ashokan Reservoir to the headwaters of the Beaverkill. After noting in 1869 in his essay "Birch Browsings," that he had seen this section of the "Catskill range" on some maps of the state, with "obvious local impropriety," called the "Pine Mountains," Burroughs was to correct this error by publishing the record of his 1885 ascent of Slide Mountain in *The Century* magazine in August of 1888. This essay, one of his most popular and enduring, was called, significantly, "The Heart of the Southern Catskills."[4]

Yet, before the 1780s, few people wished to live in the Catskill Mountains at all, and certainly not in the Southern Catskills. The Dutch, who had settled the Hudson River Valley during the mid-seventeenth century, looked to the west and its forbidding mountains with fear and antipathy in their hearts, we are told. To these lowland farmers, who were firmly planted in the rich, alluvial soil along the river, the rocky and heavily forested mountain fastness of the Catskills hardly seemed desirable terrain. Even in 1708, after the Dutch had been dispossessed by the English and eight afflu-

9

ent and well-connected individuals—among them Johannis Hardenbergh of Kingston for whom their Hardenbergh Patent was named—were granted some million and one-half acres of Catskill mountain land by Edward Hyde, Colonial Governor of New York and representative of Queen Anne, no rush to purchase or lease this land ensued. Only in locations such as Olive on the Upper Esopus Creek in 1740 and at Eureka and Lackawack on the upper Rondout Creek in 1743, for example, did sparse settlement in the Southern Catskills predate the mid-century point.[5]

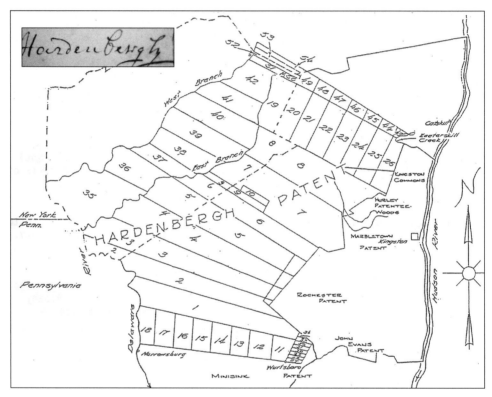

The Hardenbergh Patent. *Inset:* **Johannis Hardenbergh's signature.**
Map courtesy of Shirley Houck.

It was only in 1749, some eight years after Robert Livingston of Clermont became a Catskills' patentee, by purchasing for himself or in partnership the interests of four of the original Hardenbergh patentees, and the patent was surveyed for the second time by Ebeneezer Wooster and divided into 42 (later 52) Great Lots, that interest in this vast mountain wilderness began to develop, if slowly.[6] Land which had been locked up in litigation associated with the Hardenbergh Patent for over 30 years was now open for development. And landowners such as Robert Livingston, who had finally

**Robert L. Livingston, owner of Hardenbergh Patent lands in the
early nineteenth century, and his wife, Margaret Maria.**

obtained a map to his Hardenbergh lands, which by 1743 amounted to
about one-third of the original patent, were most interested in profiting
from them. Although these lands were isolated and heavily forested, with
no good roads reaching them, Livingston and other Catskills patentees,
nonetheless, hoped to entice land-hungry individuals to settle on them.

In this regard, the lack of roads, undoubtedly, slowed the development
of the Southern Catskills. Prior to 1765, only one road entered this area. It is
marked on William Cockburn's map of that date. This primitive road, for
much of its distance, followed the Esopus Creek. Then, it crossed the divide
between the Hudson River and Delaware River watersheds at Pine Hill and
ended in Delaware County at Pakatakan, near today's Arkville and Margaretville. In 1787 by an act of the state legislature, this road was widened
and extended to Walton, the work being completed by 1791. Also, during
the first decade of the nineteenth century, many so-called "turnpikes," both
large and small, were constructed in the Catskills. Of these, the most important to this history was financed by the Ulster and Delaware Road Compa-

ny, which was incorporated in 1802. Its "Esopus Turnpike," as it was known locally, ran from the Connecticut state line near Salisbury to Kingston, then headed up the Esopus Creek, terminating at Jericho near Bainbridge on the Susquehanna River. Built at a cost of $1,000 per mile and completed in 1806, this turnpike was opened in 1807, but was never financially successful. It was declared bankrupt in 1816, and in 1819 was taken over by the state. Just prior to this time, from 1811-1815, Abel Sprague cut the Hunter Road over the mountains from Grahamsville to the Beaverkill. An earlier road, however, from Lackawack on the Rondout Creek to Pepacton on the East Branch of the Delaware River, originally opened up the Beaverkill and predates this road.[7] It was used by marauders in 1778 during the Revolutionary War.

Nonetheless, by 1752, about 100 years after the initial settlement of the mid-Hudson Valley at Catskill, Kingston, and other sites, German immigrants, who had been recruited by agents of the patentees, began to clear the forest a bit north of present-day Monticello in Sullivan County. In addition, a limited number of settlers had already ascended the Esopus and Rondout Creeks, mentioned earlier, establishing small settlements in their valleys in the 1740s.[8]

It was not, however, until after the troubled times of the French and Indian Wars (1754-1763) and the American Revolution (1776-1783) had passed, when Native Americans, British and Tories, who had harassed the first settlers in the Catskills with such severity, were defeated, and a state of comparative safety and stability had been achieved, that the settlement of the Catskills recommenced in earnest.[9] By the mid-to-late 1780s, therefore, the pressure to settle the Catskills, dammed up for nearly 30 years, was great, and thus, once released, the first drops of what would become a wave of immigration began to flow up into the Catskills like a great human tide.[10]

In an effort to direct and to benefit from this movement, the large shareholders in the Hardenbergh Patent, such as the Livingstons, who are referred to by the historian John D. Monroe as "shrewd and acquisitive," sold outright a few small parcels of their land to pioneers who were willing to clear this land, build mills, and thus create trading centers, which would attract other settlers who, in turn, might be willing to become tenants.[11] These tenants, however, would not be allowed to purchase the land they cleared, but would lease it in perpetuity, or for one to three lives. In addition, they would agree to make an annual payment to the Livingstons and to fulfill other feudal-like restrictions to their use and tenure of this land.[12] Although rents often went unpaid and leases unofficially changed hands, and a considerable number of squatters built log cabins in the wilderness without legal right, the Livingstons' lordly control over much of the Catskills was trenchant and its maintenance firm and persistent, lasting for more than one-half century after the Revolution. According to one scholar, so arrogant were the Livingstons, that they treated their tenants "as if they were worse than...savages," and viewed them with "the deepest suspicion and disdain."[13]

In this regard, it is interesting to note that Martin Van Buren, who was to become the eighth president of the United States in 1837 and the first president elected from New York State, represented the Catskills as a state senator during a portion of the Livingstons' reign. Although Van Buren functioned as an extremely effective legislator during these years (1812-1820), his greatest contribution to the quality of life in the Catskills was to be rendered not in the august halls of government in Albany, but in the Court of Common Pleas in Hudson across the river, where, as an attorney, he defended,

Martin Van Buren defended Livingston tenants.

repeatedly and successfully, tenants of the Livingstons by limiting the police power of the Livingstons on the manor, as well as establishing the right of tenants to sell their leaseholds, when the rent and other encumbrances had been paid in full. Van Buren, who had experienced in his youth at firsthand the brazen misuse of economic and political power by the landed families of Dutchess and Columbia Counties, championed throughout his legal career the course of the ordinary person and the interests of the lease-holding tenant.[14]

Notwithstanding Van Buren's efforts, the exercise of sovereignty in the Catskills by the Livingstons was not terminated until the 1840s, when violent reaction by tenants to the injustice of a system, which prohibited one from owning the land one farms, precipitated what has been called, somewhat dramatically, but not inappropriately, the Anti-Rent War.[15]

Be this as it may, considering the cavalier attitude the patentees exhibited toward settlers and the restrictions, which they placed upon them, a surprisingly large number of pioneers from New England to the east—especially from Connecticut—from New Jersey and Long Island to the south, and even from Europe, took up the challenge of settling the re-opened wilderness and establishing farms in the Catskills between 1783 and about 1810.

Seen as the continuation of the great westward migration from Europe to the New World and across the North American continent to the Pacific

Ocean, this movement of settlers, which entered the Catskills after the Revolution, followed a pattern which continued for over 100 years, only to cease when the country had fulfilled what was unofficially designated as its "Manifest Destiny."[16] From the first settlement at Jamestown in 1609 until the Revolution, when settlers had reached Harrodsburg, Kentucky, 440 miles from the Atlantic, settlement of the North American continent progressed at a rate of approximately three miles per year. After the Revolution, until settlement reached the Pacific Ocean in the Oregon Territory in 1843, the pace increased to over 30 miles per year, ten times greater than before independence.[17] In the Catskills in the late eighteenth century, however, few, if any, settlers saw themselves as members of a national movement or migration; nor did they believe that they were participating in a great continental thrust towards the setting sun. To them, it was simply a matter of available land, and they wanted their share.[18]

CHAPTER 2
Grandeur, gloom, and solitude

IN REGARD TO THE EARLY SETTLEMENT of the Southern Catskill Mountains, William and Ann Denman are particularly interesting. For Ann and William were English, marrying seven years after the Treaty of Paris, which ended the American Revolutionary War, and emigrating to the newly formed United States of America at the end of the eighteenth century. Ann had been born in County Kent on August 9, 1772. When only 23, she and her three children—John, age four, William Jr., age two, and Elizabeth, who was less than a year old—accompanied her husband on the arduous sea voyage across the stormy North Atlantic to New York. William, who was older than his young wife, having been born in County Sussex on November 10, 1763, was in his early thirties, when he and his young family arrived in New York City in July of 1795. A "man of iron will, and strong likes and dislikes," according to his granddaughter, William also possessed an "iron constitution," which enabled him to survive the many difficulties and privations of the life of a pioneer in the Catskill Mountains.[1] In fact, William, believed to be a descendant of Vikings, or "Dane men," was to outlive his wife by 16 years, as well as two of his 11 children, dying in 1858 on his Neversink homestead at the age of 95 years.

Nonetheless, the Denmans spent an extremely trying first year in the New World. After burying their little daughter, Elizabeth, who had died in New York City in August, the Denmans, after three long months' delay, finally purchased a 200-acre parcel of land from James Desbrosses, paying

Left: **Settler William Denman.** *Right*: **An early Catskill Mountain settler.**
Courtesy of the Denman Family (left) and Hope Farm Press, a photo by Clifton Johnson (right)

10 pounds per year for eight years, in addition to paying a yearly rent of one shilling per acre. Both Ann and William signed this indenture, thus indicating that both were literate and that both were responsible for the repayment of this debt in installments. Desbrosses had inherited this and other Catskill Mountain lands from his uncle, Elias Desbrosses, who, previously, had purchased from the heirs of original patentee, Benjamin Faneuil, their interest in the Hardenbergh Patent of 1708.

The Denmans were members of a group of some 7,000 who emigrated from Europe to the United States between 1790 and 1815.[2] By 1795, four periods of British immigration had already occurred, and yet the Southern Catskills remained only sparsely settled.[3] According to the journalist and historian, James Eldridge Quinlan, settlers had only begun to enter this territory about 1788, which in 1798 would become Neversink Township in Sullivan County.[4] Even more than a quarter of a century later, the entire township of approximately 42,000 acres, including the Upper Neversink where the Denmans settled, would only reach a population of a bit more than 1,000. So inaccessible and remote was this area that Livingston land agent William Wilson, in 1802, was to refer to it as "the most abominable place on the face of God's creation."[5] It was "pathless" and "wild," the haunt of bears and "occasional panthers," said the geographer Arnold Guyot.[6] Even in 1880, in the first published history of Ulster County, Nathaniel Sylvester

Early visitors to the Catskills: Yale College President Timothy Dwight (above) in 1804 and 1815 and Henry David Thoreau, writer and naturalist, in 1844.

was to point out that the area, for the most part, remained "unimproved," with large tracts "unsettled and unsubdued."[7] And as late as the second decade of the twentieth century, the journalist and avid hiker T. Morris Longstreth, perched on top of Balsam Lake Mountain high above the Beaverkill, was to state: "Here one is at last centered in wilderness. There are no towns of any size within a day's journey. . . . A solid block of forest marches away on every side."[8]

The Southern Catskills, in fact, especially in the uppermost reaches of the Rondout and Neversink Creeks in today's town of Denning, remained in virgin forest until well into the third decade of the nineteenth century.[9] It was the last section of the Catskills to be occupied. "No one located [there] until long after the other portions of Ulster County had been settled," wrote the historian Nathaniel Sylvester. Very little land "can be reduced to cultivation." Although, he added, "along the water-courses there are a few tracts of intervale, making an occasional farm consisting of arable land."[10] But the soil was generally poor, typically "gravelly loams derived from outwash terraces" and "alluvial silt loams. . . derived from the stratified finer deposits made by sluggish waters along the flood plains."[11] With this limitation in mind, Howard Hendricks was to write in 1907, describing the neighboring Southern Catskills township of Hardenburgh: "None but the most experienced mountain farmer would be inclined to locate [here]. There is more rock and stone than soil, and there is little reason to believe that Nature ever designed it for an agricultural paradise."[12]

When Timothy Dwight, President of Yale College and scion of an old New England family, traveled through the Northern Catskills in September of 1804, he stopped at Windham. Windham had been settled some years earlier by emigrants from Dwight's home state of Connecticut. It was a civilized and Yankee-like place, very much to Dwight's liking. As he later wrote in his *Travels in New-England and New-York*, the land was "thoroughly cleared, well cultivated, and divided by good enclosures into beautiful farms." Indeed, everything, he added, wore "the appearance of prosperity." However, when Dwight looked toward the southern, more sparsely settled part of the Catskills, where the Denmans had settled less than a decade earlier, Dwight must have shuddered. For there, he was to write, he saw "nothing. . .but huge piles of mountains, separated by deep and narrow valleys." These mountains seemed to "shut out the few inhabitants. . .from the rest of. . .mankind. . . . All else was grandeur, gloom, and solitude."[13] Similarly, when the American philosopher, literary-naturalist, and author of *Walden*, Henry David Thoreau, traveled in the wilderness of Maine in the summer of 1846, he found the conditions in these backwoods not unlike those the Denmans must have experienced one-half century earlier in the Catskills. Describing this rugged and sparsely populated territory, Thoreau wrote: "this was what you might call a bran-new country; the only roads were of Nature's making, and the few houses were camps."[14] Even as late as 1876, on a camping and fishing trip to the Southern Catskills, John Burroughs was to find that things had not changed appreciably since the early days of settlement. In an essay, "A Bed of Boughs," he describes a small homestead on the Upper Neversink: "The scene was primitive, and carried one back to the days of his grandfather," he wrote, "stumpy fields, log houses and barns."[15] Upon asking a young woman, who inhabited one of these dwellings, what it was like to live deep in these mountains, Burroughs received a simple and direct answer. "Pretty lonely," she responded.[16] Not surprisingly, on his first expedition to the Neversink seven years earlier in 1869, Burroughs had himself experienced a profound sense of loneliness and isolation in this place. Remarking on its melancholy effect, Burroughs noted the pervasive "silence and. . .shadows," using a phrase hauntingly reminiscent of Timothy Dwight's earlier description.[17]

And so, it would appear that William and Ann Denman purchased their land, cited on the indenture as Farm #286 in Great Lot #5, sight unseen. For the parcel was situated high up on the side of a 3,000-foot mountain, deep in the wilderness of southeastern New York, miles from the nearest human habitation—hardly a suitable location to attempt to farm. In explanation, it could be suggested that William Denman might not have been a farmer, but an artisan. For as cultural historian David Hawke has indicated, the majority of English immigrants entering this country prior to the nineteenth century "were not necessarily farmers. . . . They came from agrarian counties. . .but most were craftsmen."[18]

Nonetheless, in the wilderness every settler, at least at first, must farm. And, thus, one wonders, whether an artisan, or even a farmer from Sussex ,with its temperate climate, cleared fields, and long-settled situation, could have imagined the extraordinary conditions under which he would attempt to farm in the Neversink during the late eighteenth and early nineteenth centuries. Clearly, it must have taken great determination, toughness, and a considerable amount of stubbornness to overcome the extreme difficulties of transporting and establishing a young and growing family in the wilderness of the Southern Catskill Mountains at this time. Certainly, what William Denman might have felt when he reached the Neversink in the fall of 1795 and began to ascend the mountain, which one day would carry his name, can only be imagined.

CHAPTER 3
Wild beasts were very numerous

OF COURSE, autumn was much too late in the year to attempt to settle in the Southern Catskills. Yet, for unknown reasons, possibly financial, instead of waiting for spring, the Denmans left New York City and headed north some 90 miles up the Hudson River to Kingston. There, long after the leaves had fallen from the trees and the first frost had occurred, William left his wife Ann and their two sons at an inn (a third son, Edward, would be born in August 1797) and took the Old Mine Road south to Napanoch, turning west and following the Rondout Creek up into the mountains to the Chestnut Woods, or Grahamsville, as it is called today. This was the nearest settlement of any consequence to the land William Denman had bought.

With winter rapidly approaching, the urgency of the Denmans' situation was evident, and the necessity to erect a shelter of some sort was critical. In November in the Catskills, when William arrived on the Upper Neversink, the temperature can often drop below freezing, and at times, there is ice and snow. It is the grayest month of the year, also, and day after day the sky is leaden.

Constructing a makeshift lean-to against a rock outcropping some 500 feet below the summit and oriented toward the southwest, William made what preparations he could. Here, the other members of his family, when they joined him, would find themselves less exposed to cold, winter winds. Today, the rock which supported the lean-to bears the inscription, "Wm.

Denman Rock on Denman Mountain.
Author photo

Denman Settled Here 1795." It is believed that about 1912, William's grandson, Aquila, and his great-grandson, William, inscribed these words on the rock. However, as recently as January 21, 1937, the *Liberty Register* states that it was Daniel Moore, whose people later bought the farm from the Denmans, who did this work. Whatever the truth may be, no trace of the lean-to, the one-room log cabin, which later replaced it, or the frame house, which was built many years later and was moved to Liberty, New York in the 1920s, can be found on the site. Only the inscription, the rock foundations of the house and outbuildings, and the perpetual spring, which nourished the Denman family for generations, remain to offer testimony to the pioneer life which was lived here long ago.

It is interesting to note that the Denmans immigrated to the United States in a time of struggle and turmoil. In 1793, two years before their departure from England, the French king had been beheaded and the infamous "Reign of Terror" had begun. France and England, too, had declared war upon each other, and Englishmen in great numbers were being conscripted into the British Navy, some even forced into service by press gangs. Given the situation in France and in England, in particular, it is not surprising that the young Denman family left England at this time.

Nonetheless, life was extremely difficult for pioneers in the Catskill

Mountains of New York State in the last decade of the eighteenth century. For one thing, most English settlers had never seen wilderness before, or experienced its rigors. According to one historian, everyone in England lived either near a country village (70%), a large town (25%), or in or near a city (5%).[1] The vast, virgin forest in which the Denmans and other immigrants settled, was the habitat of not only trout, deer, and elk—benign and familiar beings—but also of wolves, wildcats, panthers, and bear. It could be a very terrifying, as well as dangerous, place in which to live. Reports of the fearful cries of panthers, wildcats, and wolves are common in the annals of the early settlement of the Catskills. Reporting on an excursion he took to the Catskills in 1819, Henry Dwight, the grandson of Timothy Dwight, was to mention that wildcats are "not infrequent, and are often very furious," clearly "dangerous."[2] Mary Pine, who settled in Walton in nearby Delaware County in 1785, writes, "We were not without our fears. . .and wild beasts were very numerous. We often heard the wolves howl, and saw them too."[3]

Although the North American wolf, according to many contemporary authorities, is considered to be harmless to man unless injured, in the eighteenth and nineteenth centuries, this view was not widely held. The many stories of wolves following settlers for long distances through the forest, the eerie howl of the wolf, its congregation in packs, its carnivorous taste for flesh, especially that of domestic animals, and its ubiquitousness during the early years of settlement, made these mysterious and daunting inhabitants of the wilderness a fearful and troubling presence. Leah Wiltse, drawing on the memories of her pioneer ancestors to the Tannersville area of the Northern Catskills, expands on this theme, when she writes that wolves were a great menace to livestock. "For protection," she adds, "bonfires were kept burning day and night."[4]

In addition to the threat of wild, marauding beasts, the climate itself and the topography of the land offered substantial challenges to settlers. Winter comes early and lasts long in the Southern Catskills, with a frost-free growing season a month shorter than that which occurs in the Hudson Valley.[5] Much of this area, also, is situated in a "wet belt," with annual precipitation, including both rain and heavy snowfalls, amounting to between 50 and 60 inches. This is 10 to 20 inches greater than the average rate of precipitation in the Catskills in general and nearly twice the amount recorded at cities on the Hudson River, such as Catskill.[6] Due to the frequent passage across the Catskills of moisture-laden winds from the Atlantic Ocean to the south and their impedance by the Catskill Escarpment, the weather which results from this topographic feature, at times, can be extreme.[7] In March 1797, for example, less than two years after the Denmans settled in the Neversink, a violent storm devastated the area. After six days of heavy snowfall and freezing rain, on the final day of winter, a "terrific gale" developed, which blew "with unabated fury" throughout the night. This fierce, howling wind leveled thousands of acres of forest, the trees exploding and crashing to the ground under the weight of the ice and snow and the incredible force of the wind. It is reported that during this storm, people nearly went "insane," with some settlers fleeing from their cabins, fearing that they might be "crushed in their beds."[8]

Another great storm struck in August 1858, interestingly, during William Denman's 95th and last year of life. This tornado devastated the Neversink, killing three women and five children and injuring many others. One woman was lifted up and carried a distance of over 130 feet. Two children had their legs and arms broken. And a little girl nearly lost a foot and was "dreadfully cut about the head."[9]

Heavy rains, too, often occurred in the spring and fall, turning normally placid brooks and creeks into raging rivers. Settlers, who built their cabins in a flood plain, or attempted to travel during these dangerous times, did so at great peril. In this regard, Chauncey Avery and his wife, early settlers in Shandaken, the adjoining township to the northeast of the Denmans, offer a tragic example. For they had built their home on the banks of the Esopus Creek. As H. A. Haring relates the story, told to him many years after the event, one evening the Averys retired during a heavy rain, which continued unabated throughout the night. In the morning, they awoke to find their house surrounded by water, with the creek rapidly rising. It soon became apparent, that they were "cut off." So, the "terror-stricken" family climbed to the roof of the house and "held on." With an ax, Chauncey attempted to cut a nearby tree to "make a bridge to safety but the wildly rushing waters drove him back." Finally, the house was lifted from its foundation and was carried away in the raging stream, the family still perched upon it. No one ever saw the Averys alive again; for quickly, the waters "engulfed them," and they all perished—father, mother, and six children.[10]

Although with less dire consequences, the Peter Crispell family of Shandaken also suffered the ill effects of severe weather in the area. When prolonged spring rains and flooding made it impossible for them to hunt for food, and their larder became depleted, they were forced to dig up the potatoes they had planted. These rotting vegetables were all that stood between the family and starvation.[11]

Clearly, life on a Catskill Mountain homestead was difficult and dangerous. In addition to the adverse conditions created by the climate and the land, the nature of frontier life itself was precarious. Household accidents were common, with children frequently being scalded by boiling liquids or burned by falling into open fireplaces. Others were killed by farm animals, or crushed by wagons.[12] With little or no medical help available to settlers, diseases were greatly feared, with home remedies, such as roasted onion, skunk oil, or cow manure poultices, being applied for croup and chest colds, with limited success.[13] Most often, a disease was allowed to run its course. Barbara Purcell of Grahamsville relates the story of a child from the Upper Rondout Valley who, after developing pneumonia and receiving no professional care, died in her father's arms, in a sleigh during a snowstorm, on the long trip to the doctor's office, miles away in Ellenville.[14]

Flu epidemics, tuberculosis, and dreaded diseases, such as typhoid and diphtheria, periodically swept through the Southern Catskills, killing entire families, at times. During the late 1800s, in the Upper Beaverkill Valley to the west of the Neversink, many died from diphtheria, especially children. Lena Tiffany, from the Beaverkill herself, in her brief history of the area, refers to this occurrence as a "plague." A piece of red flannel tied to the door latch of a cabin indicated that diphtheria had struck, she relates.[15] Seeing this dreaded sign of quarantine, the cabin was avoided by other settlers.

Also, certain families simply seemed to possess bad luck. The family of Martin and Carrie Barnum of Maplecrest in the Northern Catskills is one such case. Of the Barnum's four children, one caught a cold and died of pneumonia. Another was born blind; a third epileptic. And a fourth, named Elmer, refused to talk to anyone but family members, remaining silent throughout his long, unhappy life.[16]

The Denmans, too, suffered similar hardships of disease and privation. During their first years in the Neversink, as with the Crispells in Shandaken, their supply of food was often inadequate. In this regard, a family story relates that, during a break in a period of repeated blizzards, William directed one of his sons to walk out of the mountains to a gristmill at Warwarsing. There, their last remaining bag of corn would be ground into meal. When the son returned home from his winter journey of many miles on foot with the precious bag of meal in his hands, his father became outraged. For the boy had brought, in addition to the cornmeal, another mouth to feed— a dog, which had been given to him on the trip. However, when the dog subsequently cornered a deer in a thicket and it was killed and eaten, the boy was forgiven.[17] Nonetheless, so difficult was it to survive in the Neversink at this time that, of Ann and William's 11 children, only two remained in this area, once they reached adulthood. And of these two children, William Jr. and Henry, Henry, the 10th child, who had taken care of his father until the old man's death in 1858, died away from home. At the time of his death in 1884, Henry had been working out for cash, peeling bark in Pennsylvania.

Chapter 4
Proficient in every handicraft

WHEN THE DENMANS AND OTHER SETTLERS arrived in the Southern Catskills, they found the land covered, for the most part, in virgin forest, or "first growth," as it is now called.[1] According to surveyors' records made about 1800, which are considered fundamentally accurate and representative today, the forest of the lower to middle altitudes of the Catskill Mountains, where settlers usually built their cabins and farmed, consisted of a mix of hardwoods and hemlock. Of these trees, approximately 50% were beech, 13% sugar maple, 7% birch, and about 20% hemlock.[2] Today, these percentages are roughly about the same, if a bit lower in regard to the hemlock, according to forest historian Michael Kudish. However, as Kudish has pointed out in recent lectures, the present extent of first growth forest in the Catskills, found predominantly in the high peaks, in contrast to 1800, cannot amount today to more than 6% of the forest population.[3]

Settlers using axes—arguably their most important tool—cleared this primeval forest by either cutting down or girdling the trees. Girdling is the process whereby a ring of bark around the trunk of a tree is removed to prevent the sap from flowing to the branches. This act eventually kills the tree, and its leaves wither, opening up the forest floor to the sun, thus enabling the first crops of corn, and later wheat, rye, and potatoes, to be planted. All wood not used for purposes of construction, or for fencing, was dragged into huge piles by oxen and burned. The resulting ashes were collected and used as fertilizer, or in the manufacture of potash (ashes mixed with water and boiled to make lye for soap or gunpowder). Potash was the settler's first cash crop.[4] During the process of clearing the land, which often took several years to complete, pioneers were sometimes injured, or even killed by falling trees, or the dropping of dead limbs.[5]

Once a small clearing was created, a cabin, built from the cleared timber, was constructed. This temporary structure, later to be supplanted by a frame house, was made of round logs chinked with split logs and plastered with clay. Floors were made of packed earth or split logs; windows were holes; the fireplace was constructed of field stone, sticks and clay; the roof of shakes or bark.[6]

This primitive, one-room structure was not the most comfortable form of habitation, however, and pioneers, especially women, who spent more time inside than men, often found it unsatisfactory. Julianna Hanford, who was born in 1875 in the Upper Rondout Valley, found her cabin "tiny, dark, almost without windows, with dirt always sifting between cracks."[7] Nonetheless, granting these sentiments, it is interesting to note, that in the

Southern Catskills, frame houses did not replace log cabins until after the Civil War, the conversion beginning in about the 1870s. And even as late as 1900, due to the high cost of paint, these frame houses remained largely unpainted.[8]

In choosing homesteads, smart settlers avoided the valleys and lowlands, preferring the uplands, fearing malaria and other fevers, which lurked where swamps and standing water existed. In addition, hillside property was not only better drained, it was also easier to clear.[9] Until the topsoil, which generally was subjected to unremitting use without crop rotation, was washed away by erosion, these hill farms, cut out of the wilderness with great human effort, were frequently fertile and productive—at least for one or two generations.

Although farms in the Southern Catskills differed in certain respects, they shared a number of similar characteristics. They were generally small, nearly self-sufficient, subsistence-based, family-run operations, often situated miles from each other, and "cut off from daily contact with the larger world."[10] Settlers bartered with each other and with tradespeople, often traveling many miles to obtain what they could not produce themselves and could not live without, such as salt. Not until well into the nineteenth century, when the Delaware and Hudson Canal was built, providing relatively cheap and easy transportation of farm and forest products, did settlers, who lived west of the plains of Shokan in the Southern Catskill Mountains, produce cash crops in significant amounts for the growing market economy, which had developed earlier in the Hudson Valley.[11]

In addition to fish and game and the fruits, nuts, and other plants, which they gathered from the wild, settlers consumed a variety of foodstuffs, which they produced themselves. Chickens, sheep, cattle, and especially swine, which were allowed to forage in the forest in summer, were a major source of protein. The hog was "the staple meat in everyone's diet," and four hogs "salted down in barrels could carry a family through the winter."[12]

Settlers also extracted syrup from maple trees, using it as a sweetener. They brewed tea from herbs, and pressed cider from apples. Most all Catskill Mountain homesteads contained apple trees, which, as John Burroughs has pointed out, "generally date back to the first settlement of the farm."[13]

Corn, however, roasted and eaten on the cob, or the kernels ground into meal for making mush, hominy grits, hoecake and "johnnycake" (a dry biscuit) was the main item in a pioneer's diet. Planted among the stumps of the first cleared trees, corn was "the staff of life for man and beast." "From no other crop would we get so great an abundance," writes this authority. "The pioneers subsisted almost entirely on this admirable grain."[14]

Early settlers' cabins in the Catskills.
Log cabin courtesy of the Delaware County Historical Assoc.; board cabin courtesy of Shirley Fulton

Although the noted New York State historian, David Ellis, has written that the settlers' method of homesteading was "predatory and inefficient," one cannot help but respect these men and women who settled in the Catskill Mountains in the late eighteenth and early nineteenth centuries.[15] For they could clear the land, build their own habitations, create and repair many of their own tools, make their own clothing, and grow most of their own food. Describing the emigration of his paternal grandparents from New England to the Catskills soon after the American Revolution, John Burroughs writes: "When my grandfather and grandmother came into the country where they reared their family and passed their days, they cut a road through the woods and brought all their worldly gear on a sled drawn by a yoke of oxen.[16] By present-day standards, such self-sufficiency and independence seems unimaginable. In the words of the nineteenth-century journalist, Ernest Ingersoll, who visited Shokan in the Southern Catskills in the 1870s, these settlers and their descendents were "proficient in every handicraft." And the women, in particular, he noted with enthusiasm, were especially "skilled" in all the "household industries."[17]

Although men and women both worked very hard, there *was* a division of labor, and each gender learned different, if complimentary, skills. For the most part, men worked out-of-doors, in the barn, in the fields, or in the forest. They tended the livestock, planted and harvested crops in season, mended fences, maintained equipment, and undertook the many chores, which kept the farm functioning. Sometimes a man might even work off the farm for all or part of a day, if the possibility of earning supplementary income developed. Women generally worked in the household. To them was given the total responsibility of food preparation, housekeeping, the care of children and the elderly and the sick, and the washing and maintenance, as well as the making, of clothing, among many other duties.

In the early years of settlement, women completed every stage in the production of homespun, or the wool and linen garments, which everyone wore. This homemade textile was called "linsey-woolsey." They scutched

Mike Todd, mountain man, 1953.
Courtesy of Evelyn Fairbairn Budd

the flax (freed its fibers from the woody parts by beating) and carded the wool by hand. Both of these items were raised on the farm. Then, they spun and wove the cloth made from these materials, and finally, they cut and sewed the final pieces of clothing.[18] Mike Todd, who was born in 1877 in Dry Brook, the next valley to the north of the Neversink, remembers: "They raised flax and spun it into a coarse thread and used it for warp—awful stout when it was twisted up tight—and they filled it in the loom with a woof of wool that had been beaten up tight, and that made an awful good cloth." He adds: "My great grandmother used to spin a lot of flax in our house. She was a short, thickset woman, and she was old; but she walked a great many miles. . .spinning yarn and settin' by the flax wheel spinning flax."[19]

Women also made soap and candles; they extracted dyes from oak and other barks, and they produced butter, which could be sold for cash. In addition, they took care of the chickens and the kitchen garden. And if they could find a few spare moments, they sewed quilts and rag carpets and engaged in other handicrafts, or went into the woods to pick berries or gather nuts, collecting these delicacies to supplement the family diet.

In the last will and testament of Cornelius P. Low of the Upper Rondout Valley, one finds a complete inventory of his property at the time of his death in 1836. Every item is carefully listed, from bedding, including a live-feather bed (plucked from live fowls) and two straw ticks, to household articles, such as baskets and a "Pepper Box." Most every item on this brief list is both useful and handmade, and significantly, a substantial portion of these objects were produced by women.[20]

During the early years of settlement, although, living difficult, often dangerous and isolated lives, settlers helped each other, shared what they possessed, and got together from time to time to enjoy themselves in each others' company. Clearly, as the historian George Tindall states, they "developed a variety of social events to combat their isolation and nurture their sense of community."[21] In this regard, in his many reminiscences of a childhood spent in the nineteenth-century Catskills near Roxbury in Delaware County, John Burroughs describes such gatherings with profound nostalgia—the house and barn raisings, the picnics on the Fourth of July with their speeches and dancing, and the much celebrated Catskill Mountain apple-cuts. Burroughs writes:

When a family was going to have an apple-cut, they sent one of the boys round the neighborhood. . . . We would arrive about seven o'clock. . . . The parers sat in the center of the room. The apples, when pared, were put in pans and passed to the rest of the company sitting around the borders of the room. Some quartered and cored them, and others would string them ready for drying. The crowd would be talking and laughing meanwhile, and jokes would be flying across the room. We cut two hours until nine o'clock. Then the apples were taken away, the room was swept up, and the boys stepped outdoors and gathered in knots to stretch and air themselves. But after a little we all got together in the kitchen again for refreshments. After we'd eaten, the amusements would begin.[22]

Churches, too, when they were built after the first difficult years of settlement, afforded places where settlers could meet and socialize. In the 1850s, baptisms took place on the Upper Rondout Creek. During these "immersions," as they were called, prospective members of local churches were sprinkled with or immersed in the creek, and large crowds frequently assembled.[23]

Admittedly, the effort it took to create a life for themselves, even at times simply to survive, was significant, and a great portion of their lives was taken up with the daily round of chores. Nonetheless, these Catskill Mountain pioneers must have experienced a sense of satisfaction and pride, when they realized what they had accomplished. For nothing like it has been attempted in the Catskills since their time.

CHAPTER 5

That thrifty and peculiar stock

OF ALL THE EMIGRANTS who came to the Catskills between the end of the Revolution and the 1820s, the most numerous and influential, by far, were the New Englanders. According to George Washington, these "inhabitants of New-England," were "continually spreading themselves."[1] In fact, during this period, more than 800,000 people from New England, one-seventh of the entire population of the United States at the time, entered New York State and settled in its upstate counties.[2] And although many of these pioneers came from Vermont and Massachusetts, the vast majority crossed the Hudson River and entered the Catskills from Connecticut. This "Connecticut hive," as it was known, was the primary source of what has been called a "Yankee invasion."[3]

Due to rapidly increasing population, overdevelopment, and the decrease of available fertile land, as well as the extensive promotional activities of large landowners, Yankees from Connecticut were prompted in great numbers to migrate to the "western countries" of nearby New York.[4] There, these transplanted New Englanders found, according to Dixon Ryan Fox, the first "paradise of speculation," in which land was bought and sold for private profit, rather than held in common by the community and distributed in the interest of the public good.[5] Place names in the Catskills, such as Windham, Stamford, Durham, and many others—all named for either townships or counties in Connecticut—as well as the distinctive New England style of clapboard architecture, offer concrete evidence of this fact.

John Burroughs' ancestors came to Roxbury from Danbury, Connecticut. Like Ralph Waldo Emerson, they epitomized, Burroughs wrote, "that thrifty and peculiar stock" of New England.[6] The Windham Valley, too, was settled by Connecticut Yankees, among them, the first to settle, we are told by a descendant, were the Hitchcocks, who came from Cheshire, Connecticut.[7] And in the Southern Catskills, Sylvester states that Samuel Merwin came from Connecticut and settled along the Dry Brook, a tributary of the East Branch of the Delaware River, before 1800. He later was joined by Hiram

Seager and Derrick Haynes. And the Todds came to this area from Connecticut, also, about 1820, it is said.[8] At this time, or a bit earlier, New Englanders, such as the Longyears and Rogers, settled along the Upper Esopus Creek in Shandaken, the Ackerleys and Lows on the upper Rondout Creek, and the Halls and Currys along the headwaters of the Neversink.

Other Yankees, probably in the 1790s, such as the Turners, the Bishops, the Hills, and the brothers William and Joseph Hollister, came to Olive along the Esopus Creek, on or near the land where the Ashokan Reservoir would be built. They all had been preceded by Dutch, German, and Huguenot settlers, such as the Brodheads and Middaghs in Olive, the Winnes and Meisners in Shandaken, and the Hornbecks and Klynes in Denning, who came to the area prior to the American Revolution.[9] Adam Eckert and his wife Jane Weeks—possibly of English descent —settled the Bushkill, just west of today's Ashokan Reservoir, in Watson Hollow near West Shokan, in 1792. Adam was descended from German Palatines, who first arrived in the Hudson Valley about 1710.[10] Farther to the west, other Yankee settlers such as the Wordens and the Stewarts, entered the upper reaches of the Beaverkill, cut clearings in the virgin forest, and constructed rustic homes.

Jehiel Stewart and his wife Rachel had heard of the availability of land and the abundance of game in this area from both the advertisements of large landholders—the Livingstons among them—and the reports of Revolutionary War army scouts, who had returned to Connecticut after the war. As a result, the Stewarts abandoned their Middletown, Connecticut birthplace in 1788, and with Jehiel's brother Luther and his family, packed up and headed west for the Catskill Mountains. That year, they reached Wawarsing in the Rondout Valley of New York State, where they wintered. The following year, they ascended the Lackawack Trail, which had been cut prior to 1785, and traveled up the Rondout Creek, crossed the mountains to the Neversink and journeyed beyond to the Beaverkill.

It was late spring, when the Stewarts finally left Wawarsing, but they used sleds pulled by oxen, even though the snow had melted; for it was easier to transport their possessions in this way. On the journey, which took two weeks, the Stewarts frequently resorted to the use of an axe; for after leaving the Lackawack Trail, which crossed the Beaverkill at Shin Creek on its way to the East Branch of the Delaware, it was necessary to cut their way through the woods, making a path for the livestock and the sleds. Before they reached their place of settlement at Big Flats—near Roscoe in today's town of Rockland, Sullivan County—where they would construct a temporary shelter of bark and poles, they were forced to cross and recross the Beaverkill many times, so difficult was the terrain. Along the way, they observed a herd of elk. And during one terrifying night, in which they heard the howling of wolves, Lydia, the little daughter of Rachel and Jehiel, somehow strayed away from camp and entered the deep woods. The profound anguish of her parents can be imagined, as they searched for their child throughout the dark night, only to find her, miraculously safe and sound, the following morning.

Nonetheless, undeterred by this harrowing experience, and by the initial isolation of the place, these Connecticut Yankees not only built their own house, but also erected a mill and established the first inn in the area, so great was their energy and their single-minded dedication, not only to survival, but also to success.[11]

Clearly, typical Yankees like the Stewarts, and the many other New Englanders who streamed into the Catskills in great numbers after the Revolution, were extremely able and self-assured individuals. John Adams, a New Englander himself, and later a president of the United States, was to describe these people, in a letter to his wife Abigail: "In solid abilities and real virtues they vastly excel in general any people upon this continent."[12]

Coming from a society long-established, which placed great stock in the values of their Puritan ancestors—thrift, hard work, and the making and saving of money—it is to be expected, that many of these ambitious individuals, once arrived in New York State, would take advantage of the distinct opportunities afforded them by a less developed and freer society. And it is not surprising, therefore, that Washington Irving, a native New Yorker, would describe, in reaction, these ceaselessly restless immigrants in highly unflattering terms. In *A History of New York*, completed in 1809, Irving writes, that these "mercurial neighbors of Connecticut" are "indefatigable speculators;" they are "marauders" and wanderers.[13] Even as late as 1889, Mark Twain was to present such New Englanders in a similar vein, in his novel *A Connecticut Yankee in King Arthur's Court*. In this work, the protagonist, an ingenious mechanic from Hartford, finds himself transported to medieval England. Possessing the infinite self-confidence and ingenuity of the typical New Englander of the time, he quickly transforms the entire society by introducing steam and electrical power. In describing

Washington Irving wrote about "Connecticut Yankees."

himself, this native of Connecticut boasts: "So I am a Yankee of Yankees—and practical." "Why," he adds, "I could make anything a body wanted—anything in the world; and if there wasn't any quick new-fangled way to make a thing, I could invent one. . . ."[14]

Unashamedly proud and outspoken about their abilities and what they could accomplish, and not always tactful in their dealings with the locals, these transplantees could seem arrogant and insensitive to the earlier Dutch, German, French Huguenot, and English settlers, such as the Winnes, Misners, Klynes, and Hornbecks, and the DuBois', Delematers, Winchells, and Crispells.

Since the early days of settlement, the boundaries of New York and neighboring states had been disputed. And as early as 1640, the New Netherlands, initially settled by the Dutch, had been pressed by its English neighbors to the east. In 1660, in fact, the New Netherlands *became* New York, and the gradual replacement of Dutch ways began in earnest.[15] Even before the inundation of New York by New Englanders began after the Revolution, the pressures exerted by New England, and especially by Connecticut, had already been felt by the older, established New York families. On June 4, 1776, for example, Robert R. Livingston of Columbia County, was to write to a relative, complaining about "those Harpies" in nearby Connecticut.[16]

Similar antipathy to a group whose political, economic, and cultural differences were clearly apparent to New Yorkers is reflected in the works of contemporary New York State writer James Fenimore Cooper. Portraying Yankees in his novels—most notably in *Satanstoe* and *The Chainbearer*—as "covetous, faithless, mean, scheming. . .and hypocritical villains," Cooper was to declare his unqualified hatred of Yankees again and again. In his creation of characters who had emigrated to New York from Connecticut—especially schoolmasters—Cooper was to expand on a character type and a theme first portrayed by Washington Irving in "The Legend of Sleepy Hollow," published in 1819-20 in *The Sketch Book*. Clearly, these characters of Cooper, especially Jason Newcombe, remind one of Irving's Ichabod Crane, whose pedantry and pretension, as well as his greedy aspiration to marry the rich Dutch damsel, Katrina VanTassel, arouses the anger of his Dutch neighbors. Returning one autumn night from a quilting party, at which his amorous suit had been discouraged by Katrina, the hapless Connecticut schoolmaster is terrorized by Katrina's jealous boyfriend, Brom Van Brunt, who, dressed as a headless horseman, drives Ichabod out-of-town, never to be seen again.[17]

A reader of psychological, as well as historical bent, might view this work as an expression of wishful thinking on the part of a disgruntled and inveterate New Yorker—a literary fantasy of sorts. Other readers, too, might even suggest that the lasting popularity of this work, which has continued to inspire numerous paintings, drawings, and films over the years, might indicate the existence of some dim, yet enduring, folk memory of the great Yankee mass migration just discussed.

However, every New Yorker did not hate Yankees; nor did every Yankee wish to move from New England to New York. Although many Yankees would migrate, significantly depleting the population of a number of Connecticut townships, many felt no interest in what were considered to be the wilder, less civilized lands to the west. Nineteen-year-old Mary Bishop Cushman was one of these disenchanted individuals. Forced to leave her friends and her beloved Connecticut home, when her family moved to Otsego County, New York, in 1795, Mary was to write in her journal: "I go to unknown lands, and leave all my heart holds dear behind. . . ." Once arrived in Otsego, although she would later accept her changed circumstances, Mary continued to measure the New York frontier by her deeply-held Yankee standards. Not surprisingly, she found its log cabin architecture, homespun clothing, and lack of cultural advantages unsatisfactory. In reaction, she wrote, "O dismal how lonesome."[18]

Nonetheless, the "invasion" of New York and the Catskills by New Englanders was to continue unabated well into the nineteenth century. And as the character of New Englandism would be modified under the new social and political conditions, so, too, was the older pattern of living in New York irrevocably changed. Without a doubt, the influence of Yankee ways on business, law, and politics, on education, and on the press in New York was "overwhelming," according to Dixon Ryan Fox. "It penetrated the whole structure of thought and all the institutions."[19] By 1821, in fact, when the New York State Constitutional Convention was convened, a majority of the 127 delegates had been born in Connecticut, or were the children of parents who had been born there themselves.[20] In addition, of the so-called "Albany Regency," which controlled the state's political machinery at the time, only one member, Martin Van Buren, was of non-New England stock.[21]

At the conclusion of the Revolution, New York State had stood seventh in population of the 13 original states. New York City was only two-thirds the size of Philadelphia and had lost nearly 600 of its homes during a war in which it had endured seven years of British occupation. One-third of all Revolutionary War battles had been fought in this state. And up and down the state's river valleys, one could find the "blackened ruins" of many "once hopeful settlements."[22]

However, once the "Great Migration" from New England began after the war, the number of people in New York increased rapidly. Between 1800 and 1820 alone, the population of New York doubled.[23] Timothy Dwight of Yale (mentioned earlier), while traveling through New York in 1810, estimated that nearly two-thirds of the people he met in New York had emigrated from New England.[24] By the late 1830s, therefore, with the aid of this deep and lasting infusion of Yankee ambition, ingenuity, and capital, New York had not only sent a native son to the White House in Washington for the first time, but had built the Erie Canal and linked the Great Lakes and the West with the sea. Truly, New York State, which had found itself in ruins only a few decades earlier, with justification and without apology, could now proudly proclaim itself to be the one and only "Empire State."

CHAPTER 6
Buccaneers and tycoons

IN THE CATSKILLS, one enterprise in which Yankee ambition, ingenuity, and capital were invested was the manufacture of leather. This process, called tanning, was to become the dominant industry in the Catskills for much of the nineteenth century. Not only would it engender a second migration to the area, creating jobs for settlers and untold wealth for some manufacturers and investors, but by opening up the forest canopy, raising the temperature of streams, changing the distribution of species of trees, and by causing erosion and the loss of topsoil, it would also alter, ultimately, the very ecology of the Catskill forest and modify the fundamental economy of the region. In fact, after the second decade of the nineteenth century, in which the first large tanneries were built on the Schoharie Kill in the Northern Catskills, tanning would sweep southward and westward throughout the Catskills, from Greene to Ulster, and to Delaware and Sullivan Counties, as the hemlock trees fell and the great groves disappeared. As a result, the Catskills, which had been wild and pristine, for the most part, up to this time, would be significantly altered, and the pattern of existence lived within them changed. As the son of tanner William Edwards was to remember somewhat wistfully in later life, the locale along the Schoharie Kill, prior to the construction and operation of his father's tannery, had been "Nearly all. . .wild land." It had abounded in "beautiful groves of hemlock timber," he was to recall. Yet, with the coming of tanning to the area, he noted sadly, all that had changed; the "glory. . .had departed forever."[1]

The men who constructed these great tanneries have been described variously, as buccaneers and "tycoons."[2] Highly eccentric, these rugged individualists, many from New England, or of Yankee ancestry, clearly, were "risk takers." They were "as acquisitive and speculative" as any entrepreneurs in our history, one historian has written.[3] Clearly, they came to the Catskills in the early nineteenth century to make money and to establish themselves in the world. In this process, many were successful, and some even created personal kingdoms.

William Edwards, just mentioned, a grandson of the famous Puritan minister, Jonathan Edwards, was a man of this sort. Arguably the first large-scale tanner in the Catskills, he had failed in earlier enterprises and had been declared bankrupt. Consequently, he came to the Catskills from Northampton, Massachusetts, to recoup his losses and to reestablish his tarnished reputation. In 1817, he built his New York Tannery on the Schoharie Kill in today's village of Hunter, later called Edwardsville in his honor. This act was accomplished with money loaned to Edwards by Gideon Lee, a prominent leather merchant and member of the New York City tanning syndicate, situated on Ferry Street near the East River, known as "The Swamp." This association of individuals, financed tanneries, supplied the raw hides to those tanneries, and sold the finished leather after it was produced. Enjoying a virtual monopoly over the manufacture and distribution of sole leather in America during much of the nineteenth century, The Swamp made the rules, so to speak, and anyone who wished to play the game followed them.

Gideon Lee, another Yankee, had been born in 1785 in Amherst, Massachusetts. As a youth, he learned to tan leather and to make shoes. In 1807, during the presidency of Thomas Jefferson, Lee moved to New York City, where he worked for William Edwards, selling the leather that Edwards produced in his Massachusetts tannery at the time. Going into business himself the following year, Lee opened a store on the corner of Ferry and Jacob Streets in New York. This store, which he called "Fort Lee," subsequently became the largest handler of leather in The Swamp. In 1817, the year he financed his old employer, William Edwards, in the Catskills, Lee formed the first joint stock company, called the New York Tanning Company. It was Gideon Lee and his fellow stockholders, therefore, who, in actuality, owned Edwards' tannery and supplied it with its first raw hides.[4] Not only a successful businessman, Lee also entered politics in later life, serving as an assemblyman, congressman, presidential elector, and as mayor of New York. President of the Shoe and Leather Manufacturers' Bank, it is said that Lee was "spare" and "aristocratic in appearance."[5] Every day he would ride his handsome black horse to the office on Ferry Street, cutting a striking figure. In 1839, Lee retired from the leather business, a very prosperous merchant, indeed. Two years later, in 1841, Lee died on his estate in Geneva, New York, in his 56th year. In the "Dedication" to his *History of the New York Swamp*, published 60 years after Lee's death, Frank Norcross was to refer to the members of The Swamp as a "galaxy of merchants such as may never again be seen." Among these men, Norcross stated, Gideon Lee had stood impressive and "gentlemanly."[6]

Norcross' praise of Gideon Lee and the other rich and powerful members of The Swamp, whom he had admired as a struggling, young journalist for the *Shoe and Leather Reporter*, notwithstanding, it is difficult today to overlook the ruthlessness of this group of entrepreneurs, among them Jacob P. Lorillard, whose name remains familiar to this day, it being printed on packages of a popular brand of cigarette. For, although Edwards was to make significant innovations to the processing of leather, even patenting his invention, and although he was to set the standard for some time for the efficient manufacture of leather, cutting the cost of production from 12 cents to 4 cents per pound through the introduction of labor saving machinery, it was these men, after all, who supplied and financed Edwards, who benefited the most from his efforts.

One must admit, of course, that The Swamp cannot be blamed completely for the demise of tanners, such as William Edwards. For tanning "was characterized by rapid turnover and frequent business failure," according to historian Richard Wiles.[7] And Edwards himself, through over-expansion and the assumption of excessive debt, consequently found himself in the same position in which he had fallen in Massachusetts 20 years earlier. Nonetheless, the power which The Swamp held over many tanners, and the control, which it maintained over the leather business during much of the nineteenth century, seems evident.

As a result of these conditions and his own mismanagement, in 1834, William Edwards, once again, filed for bankruptcy—this time in the State of New York. Far from the Catskills and their great hemlock groves, Edwards spent the last 17 years of his life in restless retirement in Brooklyn, New York.[8] One wonders, if, during these long years of urban exile, praying, reading his Bible, and writing his memoirs, Edwards ever asked himself whether, by establishing one of the first mechanized tanneries in the Catskills, and by beginning the large-scale and systematic destruction of the hemlock, he had committed an act of beneficence or malfeasance. A reading of his memoirs, however, suggests that, like many of his contemporaries, such a question never occurred to him.

To Zadock Pratt, Edwards' competitor on the Schoharie Kill, however, such ethical questions held great weight. In fact, in contrast to Edwards' seeming amorality in regard to his tanning activities, Pratt, in interviews, lectures, and in his autobiography, proclaimed the great benefits of what he had accomplished. Not only had he constructed the largest tannery in the Catskills in 1825, surpassing Edwards' New York Tannery by a considerable margin and employing some 40,000 men during its 20-year history, he had, also, built his own town.[9] Soon renamed Prattsville, this company town could boast over 100 houses, churches of different denominations, an academy, a bank (which printed its own money with Pratt's' visage emblazoned on each bill), a newspaper, a public park with fountains, and village streets with bluestone sidewalks. Of these projects, Pratt had been the primary benefactor. By 1845, when the tannery closed, this early planned community, contained over 2,000 inhabitants.[10]

Although similar in choice of occupation, these two Yankee tanners, Edwards and Pratt, clearly differed in both personality and character. Whereas Edwards was secretive and withdrawn, Pratt was open and gregarious, sharing freely information regarding his business practices, and even his trade secrets. Whereas Edwards tended to overextend himself in the conduct of his tanning business, Pratt was a model of economy and thrift, keeping exact and meticulous records throughout his long career. And whereas Edwards allowed himself to become ensnared in the clutches of The Swamp, Pratt, although he tanned hides at times for members of The Swamp, remained steadfastly independent.

A descendent of a family which had originally emigrated from England to Connecticut in the early seventeenth century, Pratt became a folk hero in his own time.[11] A tall, passionate, and unusually energetic man, Pratt was deeply proud of his strength and vigor.[12] Self-educated, Pratt reveled in the wealth and fame he had achieved. During a long and successful life, Pratt married five times—twice to two pairs of sisters, and at the age of 79, to a woman whose age he exceeded by nearly 60 years. An ardent Jacksonian Democrat, Pratt served in the State Legislature and later in Congress, where he helped to found the Bureau of Statistics, champion cheaper postage rates, promote the transcontinental railroad, and speak in favor of the completion of the Washington Monument. An enthusiast of public memorials, before his own death in 1871 at the age of 81, Pratt commissioned an itinerant stonecutter to carve a bust of himself on the rock ledges above the road just outside of town. This sculpture of Pratt, as well as of others, such as his son George, who was wounded in the second battle of Manassas during the Civil War and died some days later, can be seen to this day looking out over the countryside, which Pratt had made his own.

Unlike Edwards, Pratt cared about, and took pride in, the town he created. In its neatness and orderliness, this model village, known as "the Gem of the Catskills," was strikingly different from the many communities throughout the Catskills in which tanneries would later develop.[13] When Pratt first arrived in the area in 1824, he told the few inhabitants of Dutch and German Palatine ancestry who already lived there that he had come to live *with* them and not *on* them.[14] And this, in great measure, he had done. He was a kind and generous, if egotistical, eccentric, and quixotic patron. If asked for a loan, Pratt would examine the face and hands of his supplicant and never request collateral. Every morning, Pratt rose at 5 A.M., dressed, then walked to the tannery and breakfasted with his men. And in an act of unusual foresight and public spiritedness, strikingly absent in the history of tanning in the Catskills, Pratt even financed the establishment of a number of supporting industries in Prattsville, such as hat, mitten and glove, match, oil cloth, chair and related forest-product factories, as well as creating a model dairy farm, in order to "sustain the local economy" once the tanning era had ended.[15]

In later life, Pratt was to express extreme pride in the fact that he had planted 1,000 trees along the streets of Prattsville. Yet, he was to boast, at the same time, that he had cleared 10 square miles of virgin hemlock forest, and had tanned some million and one-half leather hides.[16] Although, as Maury Klein points out, Pratt "cared deeply for the land he stripped," and memorialized the hemlock tree in a carving incised on the rock ledges outside of town, Pratt, like Edwards and the other tanners in the Southern Catskills, with whom Pratt would later enter into partnership, seems to have been unable to assess the magnitude of the impact of his actions on the Catskills. In a long and sentimental poem called "The Tanner and the Hemlock," written by Mrs. Ann S. Stephens about seven years after the closing of Pratt's tannery, Pratt's strange and somewhat conflicted relationship with the tree which had made his fortune is presented. The poet writes: "So the tanner loves that stout old tree / With its great trunk looming there. . . ." Yet, she also writes: "Years came and went—the tanner stood / Once more by the hemlock tree / But his might had swept the gloomy wood / From the lowland, hill, and lee."[17]

CHAPTER 7
T'aint worth an interest in Shandaken

FOR QUITE SOME TIME, the generally accepted view has been that, before the arrival of Europeans in the seventeenth century, the Catskill forest was composed primarily of hemlock. So thick was this hemlock, it is believed, that, underneath its canopy, even on the brightest day, it was always twilight. One author states, in fact, that before tanning, there were "gigantic forests [of hemlock]. . .now faded away."[1] Another asserts that, when one looked at the forest from a distance, all one could see was an "unbroken blue-black color," due to the pervasiveness of the hemlock.[2] A third presumes that, before settlement, the hemlock was the most common tree in the forest.[3] And a fourth states that, prior to the building of the tanneries, the Catskills were an "almost. . .continuous forest of hemlock."[4]

Granting the authoritativeness of the sources of this opinion, it is not surprising, therefore, that such a popular view of the extent of the hemlock forest persists to this day. As a result, Robert P. McIntosh has addressed this issue in a scientific monograph on "The Forest Cover of the Catskill Mountain Region." In this pioneering work, McIntosh writes: "A common view of extensive stands of hemlock. . .is not substantiated by the data. . . ."[5] And as recent as the year 2000, in his masterwork, *The Catskill Forest: A History*, Michael Kudish finds it necessary to reiterate this view. The eastern hemlock, he writes, "is a common species in the Catskills, but it never dominated all the slopes."[6] And yet, although Kudish was to state in his 1971 doctoral thesis that "Statements that all hemlocks were cut for tanbark and that hemlocks covered the entire Catskills have been made without any serious reflection. . ." during the nineteenth century, it appeared to those who observed the destruction firsthand, that this was not the case.[7]

As early as 1851, Zadock Pratt, if somewhat self-servingly, was to write, "No more bark can be had in my vicinity. The land is cleared up for ten miles around. . . ."[8] And in his report to the Forestry Commission of the State of New York, just prior to the establishment of the Catskill Forest Preserve some 34 years later, Charles Sprague Sargent, Professor of Arboriculture at Harvard University, was to state that the Catskill forest had been so "ransacked" by lumbering and tanning interests that the possibility of yielding "merchantable timber" was "remote."[9] Even in a study of Catskill forest products released by the State Forest, Fish and Game Commission at the beginning of the next century, it was reported that "In a few years the small amount of hemlock remaining in the Catskill region will be gone, and the species will become extinct. . . ."[10] And, as late as the third decade of the twentieth century, Professor of Forest Management and Utilization at Cornell University, A. B. Recknagel, would declare emphatically that the hemlock in the Catskills "will never again play an important [economic] role."[11] This opinion would be echoed in a 1960 article, which stated that the "natural successors" of hemlock ruled out the "possibility of natural replacement of the hemlock stands."[12]

Only a Kingston newspaper publisher named A. W. Hoffman was sanguine about the matter. In 1896 he predicted that in 100 years the hemlock might return to the Catskills, the tanneries be rebuilt, and bark peeling flourish once again.[13] Setting aside the question of whether the reestablishment of the tanning industry in the Catskills is desirable, and overlooking the developments in technology which have made hemlock tanning all but obsolete, it seems evident that Hoffman's optimism regarding the regeneration of the hemlock was not shared by his contemporaries.

Nonetheless, the hemlock has proven itself to be surprisingly resilient. And interestingly, it was an ornithologist, and not a botanist, who first noted the signs of regeneration. In his study of avian life in the Helderbergs and the Catskills conducted between 1942 and 1944, Charles S. Kendeigh of the

University of Illinois was to write: "With the removal of the primeval forest, deciduous trees developed more rapidly at first, but there is nearly everywhere an abundant new growth of hemlock, so there is reason to believe that when the forest again becomes fully mature the hemlock will be as conspicuous a member of the community as in primeval time."[14] Clearly, Michael Kudish, who has spent much of his life studying the Catskill forest, has reached the same conclusion. Answering the question regarding the future of the hemlock, he writes conclusively: "Some writers of the late nineteenth century believed that the hemlock would never return. . . . This has proved to be false."[15]

However, although the hemlock did not disappear from the Catskills, vanishing like so many other plants and animal species, the tanners, nonetheless, did leave the Catskills pretty much devastated. With the supply of hemlock temporarily exhausted, hillsides denuded, burned and eroded, and with the streams polluted, sections of the Catskills looked like Georgia after Sherman's infamous march. And as the demand for leather decreased after the Civil War and prices fell, and as one economic depression followed another, tannery after tannery closed, and people began to leave the Catskills in droves. Greene County, where Catskill tanning began, was the first and the hardest hit. Between 1830-1840, Greene County had experienced a marked increase in population. And in 1845, it had produced nearly twice as much leather as Sullivan County. But by 1855, with the depletion of the hemlock in Greene County, a significant population decline had occurred and leather production had fallen to only one-twentieth of the amount produced by its Sullivan County competitor.[16] Even in Ulster and Delaware Counties, most tanneries closed in the 1870s. By then, many tanners and bark peelers, following the hemlock, had moved on to Pennsylvania and to the Adirondacks. And by 1900, according to one authority, there were only about 12 tanneries left operating in the entire state, which, at one time, had lead the Union in the production of leather.[17]

By the late nineteenth century, land, which tanners earlier had avidly sought, had lost its value. "T'aint worth an interest in Shandaken" was a commonly heard phrase at the time.[18] Nonetheless, some natives and others, who had entered the Catskills to peel bark and to work in the tanneries, invested their earnings in this forsaken land, securing hardscrabble farms for as low as 50¢ an acre. Only the most desirable land in the valleys and along the lower slopes, however, could be sold, even at this price and at terms, which were extremely liberal. Most of this land, ultimately, reverted to the counties, although some was purchased by affluent individuals at tax sales and converted into private estates or hunting and fishing clubs. Finally, legislation was passed in Albany, which released the counties from the tax debt generated by these unwanted lands, and established the Catskill and Adirondack Forest Preserves. Thus, these lands passed to the State of New York, a process, which has been chronicled in great detail by previous authors.[19] But this is getting ahead of our story.

Chapter 8
No nastier, smellier or more wasteful process

THE TANNERY ITSELF was a hive of activity. It was usually situated along a river or a stream, since abundant water was required to make the "ooze," or liquid, in which the hides were tanned. In addition, the stream itself was used as a conduit for the discharge of the noxious wastes, which the tanning process produced. It was to these places that the great quantities of bark, which bark peelers had cut, were taken.

In this regard, it is said that it took about one cord of bark to tan 10 hides.[1] And in that some 64 tanneries operated in the Catskills between the first decade of the nineteenth and the first of the twentieth centuries, many tanning thousands of hides each year, with the average life of a tannery at about 27 years, one can imagine the profound impact this industry produced on the forest and on the environment.[2] Statistics cited by one authority, for example, indicate that in one year—1868—in Sullivan, Greene and Delaware Counties, an estimated two million hides were tanned.[3]

One of the mainsprings of industrial development and environmental change in the nineteenth century, writes the historian Martin Bruegel, the tanning industry represents the "prototype of economic development [at the time] with its individual benefits and ecological costs. . . ."[4] The Prattsville Tannery, one of the largest in the Catskills, in its 20-year history, tanned some one million hides.[5] At about 10 hides per cord, this tannery would have used some 100,000 cords of hemlock bark. Thus, if it took about four hemlocks to produce one cord of bark, according to Zadock Pratt's estimate, this single tannery alone harvested the bark of at least 400,000 trees.[6] With this figure as a basis, forest historians Robert McIntosh and Michael Kudish deduce that, during the history of tanning throughout the Catskills, some seven million cords of hemlock bark must have been consumed. This means that as many as 70 million trees could have been cut.[7]

Tanning, however, was not only an extremely wasteful process, consuming prodigious numbers of hemlock trees and polluting the streams, it, also, assaulted the senses. According to Alf Evers, "It is unlikely that the human mind has ever contrived a nastier [,] smellier or more wasteful industrial process.[8] The sour smell of fermented slime, the rancid odor of untanned hides, and the stink of fish oil, permeated the tannery and often spread for miles. Without a doubt, it was a very "smelly business," writes another authority.[9]

Tanneries were also dusty. As a result, the crushed bark used to tan the hides constituted a distinct fire hazard. Thus, in many tanneries, workers were prohibited from smoking, a practice, as might be imagined, which workers abhorred.

A complex of structures, creating a plant, or factory of a sort, the tannery usually contained the largest building in town. Often measuring hundreds of feet in length and two stories or more in height, the main tannery building was an imposing structure. At the Pratt Tannery, for example, this building measured 530 feet long and 43 feet wide.[10] Composed of long bark sheds, where the bark from the forest was stored, bark mills, where the hemlock bark was crushed, and by other buildings, such as drying sheds, the tannery took fresh hides from Latin America and California, which were transported up from the Hudson River in oxcarts or in wagons drawn by mules over plank or pole roads, and turned them into rough, red leather, especially good for making harnesses and the soles of boots and shoes.

The process whereby this was accomplished was more of an art than a science at the time. And individual tanners, therefore, experimented with this age-old process, adapting it to local conditions and to their own particular requirements. In general, however, the hides were first soaked in water and pounded to soften them. Then they were "sweated" in a bath of lime and water, scraped, in order to remove all decomposed hair and flesh, and then they were placed into curing vats. Arranged in a row, these large, wooden vats, sunk into the floor of the building and measuring about six to eight feet deep, contained a solution of crushed tanbark and fresh water—usually heated—taken from the nearby stream. The hides were drawn up and down in the vats with large tongs or "vat hooks." After a specific period of time, the hides were moved from vat to vat, each vat containing an increasingly greater tanbark-to-water ratio, and thus stronger tannic acid solution. Finally, the hides were scrubbed, rolled, dried, treated with fish oil, and polished.[11]

By 1860, the Catskills yielded over seven million dollars worth of tanned leather annually.[12] And since the tanner realized his profit based on the weight increase, or the "gain," of each hide, tanning was conducted in a manner so as to maximize the absorption of the tanning solution. This process was called the "plumping up" of the hide.[13] Before the introduction of improvements to the tanning process made by Zadock Pratt, a good gain was considered to be between 16 and 30 percent. Afterwards, the increase in weight could be as much as 64 to 80 percent. At this rate, as much as 100 pounds of leather could be made from a hide nearly half that weight.[14] In addition, during the Catskill tanning era, the length of time it took to tan a

Above:
Samsonville Tannery, 1857.
Courtesy of the Olive Free Library
Historical Collection

Left:
Bark peelers.
Courtesy of William Sarles

Below:
Bark peeling.

Above: **The Dewittville tannery town, Denning Township.**
Richard Lionel De Lisser photograph courtesy of Hope Farm Press

Below: **Visitors to an abandoned bark peelers' shanty.**

Clockwise from above: **Bailey Beers, bark peeler; Col. H. D. H. Snyder, tanner; Henry Samson, tanner; Zadock Pratt, tanner.**

Beers: Richard Lionel De Lisser photograph courtesy of Hope Farm Press; Snyder: courtesy of the Phoenicia Library Historical Collection

hide decreased, from an earlier period of 18 months to 6 months.[15] However, at times, when the price of leather rose, hides could be "short tanned," that is, tanned in an even shorter time, by eliminating certain steps in the process, or by increasing the temperature of the tanning solution.[16] The leather produced in this manner was generally of a lower quality; however, through the use of technological advances, such as Col. Edwards' sole leather roller and William Tobey's bark mill, and through the introduction of more efficient practices, such as improved organization, a division of labor, and better plant design, the speed of the process could be increased and the quality, to a certain extent, maintained. Some leather, produced at first in Ellenville by Abraham Schultz, called "Union" leather, was even tanned using 90 percent hemlock and 10 percent oak bark.[17] Most Catskill Mountain leather, however, was hemlock tanned. And thus, it was highly valued, retaining its shape and color and lasting a lifetime.[18] Today, however, the role of hemlock bark in tanning has been significantly diminished; thus, not surprisingly, the quality of commercial grade leather, tanned with aldehydes, synthetic materials, and chrome, has declined.

By the late 1840s, a high percentage of tannery workers were non-natives. In fact, according to one authority, in 1855 in New York City, as many as 70 percent of tannery workers were immigrants, mostly Irish and Germans, driven to the United States by revolution in Germany and famine in Ireland.[19] Although at a lower percentage than in the city, as might be expected, the presence of immigrants in Catskill tanneries was, nonetheless, significant. Initially unskilled, these foreign-born workers had to be taught how to do the job, but they generally worked for lower pay than locals. At the Snyder Tannery, for example, in today's Woodland Valley near Phoenicia, which hired predominantly local natives, workers received between 21 and 26 dollars per month, or about one dollar per day during the 1850s.[20] However, according to the Federal Census of 1850, in its "Schedule of Manufacturers" for Greene County in the Northern Catskills, where many immigrant tanners worked, the average tanner earned only $16.29 a month. This figure amounts to about 85 percent of what a textile worker made at the time and was considerably less than that of foundry workers, carriage, furniture, and brick makers, and was less than one-half the amount earned by shipbuilders.[21]

Nonetheless, this influx of immigrant workers, as well as the many other people from outside the area who came to cut bark, work in the tanneries, or to feed, house, and supply these workers, constituted a portion of this next great wave of humanity to enter the Catskill Mountains. Mixing with the original families, who had first settled the Catskills in the late eighteenth and early nineteenth centuries, and with the Yankees, who established the tanneries and other major commercial enterprises, these newcomers, with

Left: **Claryville Tannery ruins.**
Author photo
Above: **George Erts with oxen, town of
Denning, 1890s.**

their exotic tastes and customs, their folk music and dances, their different religions, once again, as had the groups before them, not only contributed to the economic development of the area, but also added their part to the changing social and cultural configuration.

CHAPTER 9
Tanneries quickly sprang up

AS THE HEMLOCK BEGAN TO DISAPPEAR IN GREENE COUNTY, tanneries quickly sprang up to the south in Ulster County, especially in the Esopus Watershed, where large tracts of this tall, red-barked conifer flourished. Although the wood of *Tsuga Canadensis*—the botanical name for the eastern hemlock—generally is considered to be less desirable than pine for construction, being rough and coarse grained, it has been described, nonetheless, as "one of our most beautiful forest trees."[1] With "delicate silvery foliage" and "small, pendant, perfectly formed" cones, its twigs and branches being more flexible than the spruce and fir, the hemlock reflects sunlight and can sway in the wind, often moving the observer in profoundly deep ways.[2] Growing at times to a height of well over 100 feet, and reaching diameters of from three to eight feet, the eastern hemlock has been known to live to an age of between 300 and 400 years. This fact makes the hemlock one of our most venerable local organisms.

By the fourth decade of the nineteenth century, therefore, in today's townships of Olive and Shandaken, a number of tanneries were constructed on the Upper Esopus and on adjacent streams. In fact, it has been estimated that at least 13 tanneries were built along the Esopus and in the Ashokan basin between 1831 and 1856, with four additional tanneries having been established prior to these dates.[3] In the township of Shandaken alone, there were eight tanneries. At Pine Hill, Augustus A. Guigou built his Empire Tannery in 1831. And about two miles down Birch Creek below this tannery, Isaac Smith operated a tannery from 1844 until the 1860s. Prior to emigrating to the United States from France, Augustus Guigou had served with Napoleon and had crossed the Alps with the general's forces on one of his campaigns.[4]

Another tannery, which in its last years would be known as the Wey Tannery, was established in 1835 by Robert Humphrey in Big Indian. It stood about a mile below what would become the Ulster and Delaware Railroad depot.[5] The source of hemlock for this tannery, which closed in about 1870, was the Big Indian Hollow, mainly virgin forest at the time. Up Bushnellsville Creek, just south of the county line, A. Bushnell built a tannery in the 1830s, which closed sometime after 1856. And to the east and closer to Phoenicia along the north bank of the Esopus Creek at Fox Hollow, Charles and Giles Isham built a tannery in 1835. Subsequently, in 1840 and 1845 respectively, George Palen and Eliakim Sherrill became partners in this tannery. Although the tannery would be sold to Hiram Whitney in 1857 or 1858, and after its closing at the end of the Civil War would become the Whitney Chair Factory, the tannery itself has become known as the Sherrill Tannery. Col. Eliakim Sherrill served in Congress from 1847 to 1848 and, during the Civil War, raised the 126th Regiment. Sherrill was wounded at Harper's Ferry and later died during the Battle of Gettysburg on July 3, 1863.[6] Mt. Sherrill in Shandaken is named for this man.

In this regard, it is interesting to note the high level of patriotism and sacrifice exhibited by Catskill Mountain tanners and their families during the Civil War. It may be remembered that Zadock Pratt and his wife lost their son to this war. The son, George Pratt, had previously become a tannery owner himself in 1853, when his father gave him the tannery at Samsonville.

Near today's village of Phoenicia, two tanneries were built. Col. H. D. H. Snyder built one in 1851 in Woodland Valley. It closed in 1865. Most notable, however, was the Phoenix Tannery, which would give its name to the local hamlet. Just above the confluence of the Esopus and Stony Clove Creeks in 1836, two men named Moore and Ellis built this tannery, which operated until 1870.

James A. Simpson, who later owned the Phoenix Tannery, like Zadock

Pratt, was known for his eccentric behavior. As Kingston newspaper-man A. W. Hoffman tells the story, both Simpson's brother and father had died of tuberculosis, a common cause of death in the nineteenth century. And so, when James himself was diagnosed with the disease, he realized that he must do something quickly or die. During the nineteenth century, before the discovery of miracle drugs, tuberculosis was treated primarily with sun and fresh air. To restore the health of one's lungs, it was believed, breathing pure air, especially mountain air filled with the fragrance of evergreen trees, was essential. With this belief in mind, Simpson decided to improve upon the standard treatment. In fact, he would attempt "a novel cure." Forthwith, Simpson directed his carpenters to build an airtight room above the tanning vats in his Phoenix Tannery. Into the floor of this room he ordered holes to be bored, so that the fumes of the tannin from the vats could rise and fill this special compartment. Simpson, then, tenanted this room for a part of each day. As a result, it is said, he was cured completely. Not surprisingly, from this time forth, Simpson was known throughout the Catskill Mountains as the man who had tanned his own lungs.[7]

Farther to the east, beyond the Ladew Tannery, which was built at Mt. Tremper in the town of Shandaken sometime between 1840 and 1846 and closed in the 1860s, tanning was also conducted.[8] Here, in the town of Olive, primarily on the Esopus and its tributaries, but also on the Mettacahonts Creek, a total of nine tanneries were built. They were constructed between 1810 and 1856—one in Boiceville, one in West Shokan, one in Shokan, three in Olive City, two in Tongore (today's Olivebridge), and one in Samsonville. Of these, the most notable were the Metropolitan Tannery in Watson Hollow near today's West Shokan and the Palen and Hammond Tannery in Palentown (today's Samsonville), later called the Samson Tannery.[9]

The Metropolitan Tannery was built by Nathan W. Watson, a Yankee from Canaan, Connecticut, about 1856. Watson owned or obtained the bark rights to extensive acreage in the Southern Catskills during the last half of the nineteenth century. In the township of Olive, where his tannery was located along the Bushkill Creek, and also in the adjacent townships of Denning and Shandaken, Watson stripped the bark from the hemlock in over 9,000 acres, cutting deep into the Moonhaw and up Balsam Cap, Friday, Cornell, and Wittenberg Mountains.[10] Granting the size of his holdings, it is not surprising that the impact of Watson's activities in this part of the Southern Catskills was profound. The effect of cutting and barking all hemlock at least one foot in diameter up to elevations as high as 2,600 feet can only be imagined.[11] Clearly, driving bark roads deep into the Peekamoose, an area only sparsely inhabited at the time, undoubtedly, changed the nature of local pioneer life and altered the forest ecology of the region. On a fishing trip undertaken in 1876 to the Rondout Creek near Peekamoose,

John Burroughs was to confirm this fact. Ascending Peekamoose Mountain above today's Peekamoose Lake, the naturalist was to remark with dismay, "our course was along the trail of the bark-men who had pursued the doomed hemlock to the last tree at the head of the valley."[12]

Politically active, as were many Catskill tanners, Nathan Watson served as supervisor of the town of Olive a number of times between 1850 and 1866, and also sat as a member of the New York State Assembly in 1857. During its years of operation, it is said, his Metropolitan Tannery employed some 100 workers, both at the tannery, in the woods, and on the road. The tannery, it is believed, burned during the winter of 1870, although other sources give the years 1865 and 1873, and another believes that the tannery did not burn at all, but simply closed in 1866 and was converted into a saw and heading mill, which seems possible.[13] Whatever the case, little trace of the Metropolitan Tannery remains today. Only the stone base of the tannery chimney and a hole, indicating the location of a large building along the Bushkill Creek, can be detected. This may be explained by the fact that, during the early twentieth century, stones from the tannery foundations were used to build Ulster County Route 42, the Peekamoose Road.[14] Also, according to local historian De Witt Davis writing in 1907 some 30 to 40 years after the closing or burning of the tannery, "Watson Hollow was formerly the center of active business." There was "a large tannery" there, "now gone," and "many of the houses have been torn down" and the people moved away.[15]

Across the mountain from the Metropolitan Tannery on the southeastern side of Mombaccus Mountain, stood the Palen and Hammond Tannery. Constructed in 1831 on the Mettacahonts Creek in Palentown (today's Samsonville), this tannery during its history was owned by a number of individuals, in addition to Palen and Hammond. Among them were a man named Edson, Hewett and Peter Boice, Zadock Pratt and his son George, as well as General Henry A. Samson, a highly respected local citizen and "business man of boundless energy," whose name has been associated with this tannery as well as the hamlet in which it was built.[16] Flourishing for more than 30 years, the Samson Tannery, as it became known, was one of the largest in the Catskills. Until the bark on the slopes of High Point and Mombaccus Mountains and up through the Balsam Swamp to Sundown disappeared and the price of leather fell, the Samson Tannery processed even a greater number of hides and consumed even more cords of hemlock bark in its longer history than did the Pratt Tannery, its predecessor in Greene County.[17] With its sizeable population and the benefit of the tannery's substantial payroll, Samsonville, in the mid-nineteenth century, became the "largest and most prosperous" hamlet in the Catskills.[18]

A lithograph of Samsonville and the Samson Tannery dated 1857, when the tannery was operated by George Pratt and Henry Samson, depicts an extremely large complex of multi-storied buildings, long storage sheds, and a tall chimney tower, all situated at the base of the mountain in a pastoral setting of cleared fields, ample farms, and a charming and settled village.

Sometime after the end of the Civil War, however, the tannery ceased to produce leather, and in 1873 it was converted by Pratt Shurter into an excelsior mill. By 1880, the site had been abandoned. Experiencing a similar fate to that of other boomtowns in the Catskills, Samsonville, after 1880, fell into decline.[19] Although the tannery buildings had been consumed by fire and rebuilt twice previously, in 1882 they burned to the ground once again, and were never rebuilt.[20] Today, little evidence of Samsonville's glory days remains. Along the Mettacahonts Creek where the great tannery stood, those who search carefully will find mainly stone foundations, poison ivy, and tangled vines.

Roughly eight to ten miles to the west of the Metropolitan Tannery as the crow flies, but considerably farther by primitive road, three important tanneries existed. These tanneries were built beyond Peekamoose and over Red Hill in the valley of the East Branch of the Neversink. Originally part of the Hardenberg Patent of 1708 and the last section of New York State to be settled other than the Adirondacks, the lands surrounding these tanneries remained for the most part a wilderness, even after they were surveyed and partitioned into Great Lots 5-7 in 1749. Although early settlers to the area, such as the Denmans and the Currys in 1795, and later Anthony Schwab and Steven Van Dover in 1841 and 1842 respectively, would cut farms out of the virgin forest on the mountainsides above the East Branch of the Neversink, little development occurred here until the advent of the tanneries.

However, prior to the construction of these tanneries, many investors already had owned these lands, hoping to profit from them in some fashion. First among these individuals were the original Patentees of 1708, Benjamin Faneuil and Johannis Hardenbergh. In the lottery, which followed the survey and partition of the Patent in 1749, Faneuil drew Great Lot 5, and the designees of Hardenbergh, who had died the previous year, Great Lots 6 and 7. Over the years following this apportionment, and before the American Revolution, these lands changed hands many times, going to members of the New York landed gentry, such as Elias and later James Desbrosses, Guilian Verplanck, and Robert Livingston.[21]

In the early nineteenth century, these lands became the property of businessmen and entrepreneurs, such as William Denning, who in 1828 bought at tax sale for less than a cent an acre over 20,000 acres previously held by a Philadelphia land grant corporation. Ten years later, this land within Great Lots 6 and 7 passed to William H. Denning. A Hudson River brickyard owner, Denning, for whom the town of Denning was named later in 1849 when it was created out of the town of Shandaken, subsequently added to these substantial holdings in the Southern Catskills. As a result, by 1841, Denning held title to more than one-third of the land in the future township.[22] Arranging that his property be mapped and surveyed by Stephen Royce, Denning began offering his land for sale between 1839 and 1841.[23] It was, therefore, from investors, such as William H. Denning, that those who built the Upper Neversink tanneries, between 1848 and 1849, purchased the right to cut timber and to strip the bark from the hemlock.

Farthest up the Neversink in the hamlet of Denning in Ulster County, John W. Smith built a tannery, which was operated subsequently by Pierce Brothers and later Johnson Brothers until 1885. A bit downstream in Dewittville, L. Hammond and Company, and later Dewitt and Reynolds, also ran a tannery until somewhere between 1880 and 1885. And finally, just below where the East and West Branches of the Neversink meet at Claryville in Neversink Township of Sullivan County, the third Upper Neversink tannery, which would be remembered as the Claryville Tannery, was established. Built in 1848 by James V. Curry, or on land owned by Curry, who named the area for his wife Clarissa, this tannery was the largest in the Upper Neversink, employing about 50 men, and tanning annually some 30,000 hides.[24] Owned for much of its history by Snyder and Bushnell, this tannery was later purchased by Cook, Bushnell and Reynolds. A historical plaque marks the site of this tannery in Claryville, where some interesting and extensive ruins, including a beautifully constructed stone chimney, can be found.[25]

Before becoming a partner in the Claryville Tannery, it is interesting to note, John Reynolds had served as Bushnell's bookkeeper and later tannery superintendent. In about 1867, Reynolds, a rising entrepreneur, had bought the Hammond Tannery in Grahamsville, renaming it the Grahamsville Tannery. After the Depression of 1873, however, this tannery lost money each year. And in 1878-1879, about the time the Claryville Tannery closed, Reynolds went bankrupt. As a result, Reynolds lost everything he owned. Ironically, at the time, the Grahamsville Tannery storage sheds had been bursting with finished leather and its yard filled to overflowing with hemlock bark amounting to hundreds of cords.[26]

To all of these tanneries, hides were brought from the D & H Canal in Napanoch. Transported by teamsters, their big wagons drawn by many mules, men such as Barney Richards, were "the wonders of that day."[27] After 1855, the hides were brought to the tanneries and returned to the canal as leather over the Napanoch and Denning Plank Road. It was constructed using lumber from the many hemlock trees, which the tanneries had cut. When these Upper Neversink tanneries closed in the 1870s and 1880s, life changed dramatically in the area. As one observer put it, describing

Dewittville in the 1890s, "since the tannery. . .ceased to operate and the tidal wave of prosperity, which that business brought into the place retreated. . . this 'little hamlet' has been left 'high and dry'."[28]

Among the 39 tanneries situated in Sullivan County at mid-century—the greatest number within a county in New York State at the time—L. B. Babcock and Company and S. Hammond and Sons should be mentioned, if only briefly, because of their proximity to the tanneries just discussed. The Babcock Tannery, standing to the northwest of Claryville, was established by Linus Babcock on the Beaverkill, either in 1832 or 1840—there is some disagreement. It was later purchased by William H. Ellsworth and James Murdock in 1862 and processed some 20,000 hides, consuming about 2,000 cords of bark annually. The only tannery built on the Upper Beaverkill, this establishment burned to the ground in about 1887. The site of this tannery can be found just below the covered bridge in the present Beaverkill State Campground.[29]

Situated at the meeting of the Willowemoc and Mongaup Creeks about eight miles to the west of Claryville in the hamlet of Debruce (or DeBruce, named for the early landowner Elias DesBrosses or Debrosses), the Stoddard Hammond and Sons Tannery was built. Constructed by Stoddard Hammond and James Benedict in 1856, this tannery held the rights to cut bark on some 35,000 acres. Operational for at least 15 years and most probably longer, this tannery tanned some 60,000 hides a year. Consuming some 12,000 cords of hemlock bark each season, it may have been the largest tannery in Sullivan County at the time.[30]

In the 1840s, when the Upper Neversink tanneries were established, much of interest would occur in the Catskills and in the nation. During this time, Henry David Thoreau would visit the Catskills in July of 1844, finding at South Lake and the Kaaterskill Falls the inspiration for his momentous experiment at Walden Pond. Also in 1844, the Anti-Rent War would erupt in the Catskills, mentioned previously, which would culminate in the State Constitutional Convention of 1846, when the Constitution would be revised and, in effect, the manorial system would be abolished. In 1848, James Marshall, a carpenter from New Jersey, would find a gold nugget smaller than a pea in a millrace on the American River in California. And this seemingly simple act would prompt nearly 100,000 prospectors, over the next four years, to travel across the continent or around the Horn in search of wealth—doubtless, some of these individuals would come from the Neversink. And in the same year, the Seneca Falls Convention would take place. Called by Lucretia Mott and Elizabeth Cady Stanton, this momentous meeting of women would issue its "Declaration of Sentiments" and its "Resolutions," stating, in part, that "all men and women are created equal" and that women possessed the right to intellectual and political equality, to vote, to speak at public assemblies, to gain an education, and to engage in all trades, occupations, and professions.[31]

CHAPTER 10
Pretty hard sort of grub

WHEN YOUNG JIMMY DUTCHER hiked over the mountains from Prattsville to Shandaken in 1851, he was not traveling for pleasure; he was looking for work. His father had died two years earlier; his mother had remarried, and life had become tough for Jim at home. So, Jim—13 years old at the time—left his family and set out in the world on his own. The Pratt Tannery in Prattsville, where Jim had lived, had been closed since he was seven. However, to the south in Ulster County, bark was being cut in the Big Indian Valley in great quantity. Here, the Wey Tannery held the rights to a vast acreage, which took in both sides of the valley and climbed up the notch to the headwaters of the Esopus Creek. Like many other folk from the Northern Catskills, where the hemlock bark had been depleted, Jim headed south and found work.

At first, Jim gathered bark for a bark contractor, but within four years, he had become a contractor himself, entering into agreements in his own name at the age of 17. In later life, Jim would regale avid listeners with stories of the days he had spent as a young bark peeler in the Big Indian Valley. "For a mile and a half up the valley the timber had been cut along the stream," he remembered, "but above that there was unbroken hemlock forest that axe had never touched."[1] Living in accommodations provided by the contractor deep in the forest, Jim found conditions a bit difficult. The hut, in which Jim ate and slept, measured only 16 by 20 feet. It had been constructed hastily of hemlock wood and bark, since it would soon be abandoned, as the hemlock retreated and the bark peelers moved up the valley. Inside this shanty, as these temporary structures were called, Jim found two beds, a stove, benches and a table, all rough-hewn. Into this little bark shanty were crammed the owner and his wife, their six children, four bark peelers, a pack of dogs, and an animal, which greatly surprised Dutcher. For underneath the ladder which provided access to the upstairs loft, where Jim slept on the floor with the other bark peelers, was chained a large black bear. "I tell you," Jim stated, "my eyes stuck right out when I see that bear, for I had come down from Prattsville, where there was a village."[2]

The food, too, provided for bark peelers by the contractor was not always good, or even sanitary, for that matter. Jim remembers how, in that bark shanty, the wife had cooked their dinner, "smoking a pipe over the kettles."[3] Sometimes, even, the food was spoiled. A humorous blessing given at the time, memorializes the poor quality of butter placed on the table by a contractor named Conrad. It states: "Oh Lord of Love/Look down from above/And give us something better/We're crammed and jammed and daily damned/With Conrad's stinking butter."[4] Bailey Beers, mentor and friend of Jim Dutcher, and a bark peeler himself in the Neversink, also remembered that they had a "pretty hard sort of grub in them times and durned few of the bark peelers saw fresh meat mor'n once or twice a year."[5] Most of the time they ate salt pork or trout caught in the streams. And on the weekends, to supplement this limited diet, they might dig out a woodchuck, or shoot a raccoon.

The bark cutting season took place in the spring and early summer. This was the time, when the sap flowed in the hemlock trees, and the cambium layer between the outer bark and the wood became soft. This soft layer was called the "slime." Before the slime hardened in July, the bark peeler could remove the bark easily with a tool called a spud. This barking iron, which looked like a thin spade or shovel, possessed a spoon-shaped blade at its end, and according to one old-timer, was a tool to respect. It was "a wicked thing, a good heavy one with a blade onto it."[6]

After a ring was cut at the base of the tree and another four feet above it, with a short-handled hatchet, which hung from the belt of the bark peeler, the bark was removed with the spud in 12- to 16-inch-wide sections. Then, the tree was felled with an axe, and the remaining bark was removed up to the first big branches in four-foot lengths. Only a small portion of the tree was used. Generally, the rest was left to rot where it fell. Afterwards, the cut bark was either piled in the woods, bark side up to prevent curling, taken out to the nearest road, or was hauled to the tannery, where it was stacked in large drying sheds, some over 100 feet long. The farther the bark was hauled, the more the contractor charged. After paying their expenses, contractors hoped to realize at least $1.00 to $1.25 profit a cord (a pile 4 x 4 x 8 feet). According to meticulous records kept at his Prattsville Tannery, Zadock Pratt routinely paid on the average of about $3.00 for each cord of bark delivered to the tannery.[7] Most hauling was done in the winter, when the bark, stacked on sleds, could be more easily dragged over the ice and snow. In this endeavor, many teams of horses and oxen were used.

Bark peeling was extremely difficult and dangerous work. At any moment, a branch or tree could fall and crush a man; a misstep on a slippery tree trunk could result in a broken bone, or a sharp-edged tool could slip and cut a deep wound. Working, as did Jim Dutcher, from sunrise to sunset, approximately 15 to 16 hours in the spring, the bark peeler was paid between $1.50 and $2.75 a day, but some bark peelers made less.[8] Although anything over $1 a day was considered good pay at the time, and the peeler's credit at the local tavern or general store was assured, it was expected that he would peel and pile about two cords of bark in a day—no easy task for anyone.[9]

The clothing of bark peelers quickly became impregnated with sticky slime. As a result, leaves and twigs stuck to their shirts, and their trousers became so heavy and rigid with sap, it is said, that they could be stood against the wall at night. Insects, too, were the bane of these workers. For in the spring, when the bark was peeled, black flies, newly hatched, were thick, and bit voraciously any exposed patch of skin. "They'd just kill you in warm and cloudy weather," states Mike Todd, whose grandfather had cut bark. "You'd douse your face with kerosene and tar."[10] At night, smudge fires were lit, in order to allow the workers to sleep. But this practice did not always work, and it filled the bark shanties with suffocating smoke. At times, the bugs were so bad, that men slept with their heads stuck into feed sacks.[11] As a result of these conditions, bark peelers were tired all the time and often displayed a haggard and exhausted look. One bark peeler remembers his days in the woods. He writes: "At no other work in the forest did we suffer tortures of so many kinds. We panted for breath in the dead, hot air of the closed-in glades in which hemlocks choose to grow; swarms of mosquitoes found their way to every part of our thinly clad bodies; black flies chewed the flesh and raised great welts."[12]

In early July, these torments finally ceased, when the bark-peeling season came to an end. And throughout the Southern Catskills on July 4, both the birth of the nation and the end of this season were celebrated with enthusiasm. Out of the depths of the forests came exhausted, but now affluent, bark peelers, who, once they reached civilization, drank large quantities of alcohol, fought each other lustily, and generally had a riotous, good time. Everyone, however, did not approve of such practices, nor even of these hardworking men. Horace Greeley, for example, the noted social reformer, presidential candidate, and publisher of the *New-York Weekly Tribune*, bemoaned this situation. Calling bark peelers, "shiftless," he asserted, that "poverty, lack of education, irreligion [and] love of liquor" were their hallmarks.[13] In a contemporary restatement of Greeley's assessment of bark peelers, Leah Showers Wiltse, a descendent of pioneers in the Northern Catskills, writes, "Every spring, a horde of bark peelers came into the mountains, staying as long as the bark could be peeled from the trees. . . ." She continues, "By midsummer, their task done, most began to drift away. With few exceptions [they] contributed little to the advancement of civilization."[14] Yet, as if to balance this one-sided view, economic historian Richard Wiles points out, that bark peeling was "casual," "seasonable" employment, with "'moving on' an everyday occurrence."[15] And, as the editors of *Folk*

Songs of the Catskills more fairly state, "the drudgery of transient occupations," such as bark-peeling, "left little time or strength or opportunity for a broadening of the human vision."[16] Thus, granting the nature of the work and the conditions under which it was performed, it is not surprising that, when given the chance, these workers engaged in such rough-and-tumble diversions.

CHAPTER 11

A product of the mountains

ALTHOUGH JAMES W. DUTCHER, OR "JAMES WALTON," as he is referred to by his descendents, knew well the pleasures and the pain of the bark-peeling season, having spent more than 20 years in the woods as a bark peeler and contractor, it is for his other endeavors and accomplishments, however, that Jim is best known. Marrying Mary Andrews in 1860, the daughter of a transplanted Yankee from Connecticut (Jim's mother had been a Connecticut Yankee, too), Jim and Mary produced 11 children, two dying in the same year of 1883. Together, Mary and Jim built the Panther Mountain House in the 1870s at the head of the Big Indian Valley, which Jim's work as a bark peeler had helped to clear. Here, Jim farmed, operated the boarding house with his wife, was appointed postmaster in 1880, and became a mountain guide of wide renown. In the *Commemorative Biographical Record of Ulster County, New York*, published in 1896, it is asserted, that Jim was "the best known and most reliable guide" in the Southern Catskill Mountains at the time.[1]

Jim began leading groups of summer boarders up Slide Mountain in the 1870s, about the time the local tanneries were closing down. He blazed a trail up the mountain, built the first observation tower on the summit, and added the stone steps in difficult sections, which, if in some disrepair, are used to this day.[2]

Referred to as "the guardian spirit" of Slide Mountain in his later years, when Jim Dutcher first came to the Southern Catskills to cut bark, he "didn't know much," according to Bailey Beers, his mentor and friend.[3] However, in time, Beers was to admit, Jim "got to be quite a lad."[4] Gregarious and convivial, Dutcher liked to dance and sing. Photographs taken of Dutcher in the late 1890s by the itinerant photographer, Lionel De Lisser, evidence these exuberant qualities. In two of these highly engaging images, Jim, dressed dashingly in white shirt and black swallowtail coat, carrying a long walking stick, jauntily guides a party of some eight women up Slide Mountain, a pipe gripped firmly between his teeth. In another photograph, Dutcher is pictured deep in the wilds of Panther Mountain near Giant Ledge. Here, he guides four urban hunters, all carrying guns. Dutcher, in the foreground, sips from a small, brown bottle, a broad smile on his face.[5] After meeting and photographing the "old hunter and guide," De Lisser was to write, he is "a product of the mountains, such as only the mountains can produce."[6] Or, as Jim's granddaughter has said, "Grandpa was a free spirit. He did his thing his way."[7]

The photographer Richard Lionel De Lisser, like James Dutcher, was also an interesting person in his own right. Traveling throughout the Catskills in the 1890s in a buggy drawn by his elderly but faithful horse, "Cherry-Tree," De Lisser methodically photographed all persons and places of interest. The result of this odyssey was collected in two books. In 1894, the Picturesque Publishing Company of Northampton, Massachusetts published his trip to the Northern Catskills of Greene County, called *Picturesque Catskills*. And between 1896 and 1905, in eight numbers, or volumes, which covered De Lisser's trip to the Catskills in Ulster County, a group of local businessmen published *Picturesque Ulster*. This latter work, which includes a prose narrative of De Lisser's trip, called "The Artist's Ramblings," is not only an invaluable historical resource, containing stunning pictorial images and the oral record of the folkways of a culture now lost, it is, also, an enduring work of art.

An accomplished landscape painter, as well as a professional writer and photographer, De Lisser was born in New York City—probably in the late 1840s—studied art in Germany, and came to the Catskills on assignment in 1893 to pursue the project which would become his lifework. A mature and experienced artist at the time, De Lisser's carefully observed and meticulously rendered photographs, taken with his large and heavy mahogany and brass camera, present and preserve with impeccable artistry and craftsmanship, as well as with "rare and genuine sympathy," the "honest and simple way of life" of local folks in the Catskills at the end of the tanning era.[8]

Although De Lisser's humorous and relaxed writing style suggests an optimistic and buoyant personality, De Lisser was deeply depressed, nonetheless, by the lack of financial success of *Picturesque Ulster*, which sold for only 75 cents per volume, and whose publication was suspended by Styles and Bruyn of Kingston before the last two projected volumes could be completed. Although the poor sales of De Lisser's masterpiece can be attributed not to the quality or importance of the work, but to distribution problems and to strong competition initiated by the railroads, which distributed free pictorial promotional materials in vast quantity to tourists, the failure of *Picturesque Ulster*, it is believed, contributed to a marked decline, after 1905, in De Lisser's health.[9] Abandoning the project with regret, De

Jim Dutcher and hikers descend the step trail in the 1890s and the step trail today.
Richard De Lisser photograph courtesy of Hope Farm Press; right—photograph by Rowland Dutcher

Below: **Giant Ledge hunting party with Jim Dutcher as guide.**
Richard Lionel De Lisser photograph courtesy of Hope Farm Press

The lower observatory on Slide Mountain.
Richard Lionel De Lisser photograph courtesy of Hope Farm Press

Below: **The summit of Slide Mountain, the Catskills' highest peak.**
Richard Lionel De Lisser photograph courtesy of Hope Farm Press

Slide Mountain summit campground, Jim Dutcher, guide.
Richard Lionel De Lisser photograph courtesy of Hope Farm Press

Below: **Jim and Mary Dutcher's Panther Mountain House.**
Richard Lionel De Lisser photograph courtesy of Hope Farm Press

Lisser left the Catskills, which his photographs would immortalize, never to return again. In the futile hope of regaining his failing health, he returned to Munich, Germany, where his artistic career had begun. But, sadly, his search for rejuvenation through a change of scene was unsuccessful. And in September 1907, Richard Lionel De Lisser died in Munich in middle age. Coincidentally, but significantly, in the same year, the Mayer Tannery closed in Shokan. It had been the last tannery to operate in the Catskills.[10]

Chapter 12
That feller Bryan

IN 1896, however, when they first met, Richard Lionel De Lisser and James W. Dutcher were both active and healthy. As eccentric and unpredictable as he was able and enterprising, Dutcher, throughout his life, maintained passionately held political beliefs. An ardent Republican, Jim had been appointed postmaster of Slide Mountain by President Rutherford B. Hayes. And when Jim learned one summer day in 1896 that William Jennings Bryan, the Democratic candidate for the presidency, would soon visit the Winnisook Club at Helsinger Notch at the head of the Big Indian Valley, not far from Jim's own Panther Mountain House, he was deeply disturbed.

Fresh from the Democratic National Convention in Chicago, where Bryan had delivered his famous "Cross of Gold" speech, the 36-year-old, ex-congressman from Nebraska, with his spellbinding style of oratory, was crisscrossing the nation, at the time, in a whirlwind campaign. In the three months prior to the election, Bryan would not only enter the Southern Catskills, but also would cover 18,000 miles and deliver an unprecedented 600 speeches.

When Jim Dutcher discovered that Bryan's trip up the Big Indian Valley to Winnisook was imminent, he remarked, it is recorded, "We'll show that Bryan feller how we stand."[1] And so, stringing a McKinley and Hobart banner across the road on which the Bryan delegation would pass, and taking up a strategic position nearby carrying his trusty shotgun, Jim awaited Bryan and his supporters with a determined look upon his face. It is not recorded how Bryan reacted to Jim's demonstration of political opinion, or whether he responded at all. Certainly, the "Great Commoner," as he was called, seems, in general, to have been impervious to negative criticism. What *is* known about the visit, however, is that Bryan, the next day, left the Catskills disappointed.

Founded about 10 years earlier by prominent New York State Democrats, among them Thomas E. Benedict, head of the United States Printing

Presidential candidate William Jennings Bryan and his wife, Mary.

Office, and Judge Alton B. Parker, who would run for the United States presidency in 1904, the Winnisook Club was chosen by Major Hinkley, the Chairman of the State Democratic Committee, as the site for the meeting with Bryan. Although he was an ardent Democratic, Hinkley, a member of the Winnisook Club, was not a supporter of Bryan, nor of his policy of free silver. And thus, Hinkley selected the setting of this private and informal hunting and fishing club, deep in the wilderness of the Southern Catskills, to discourage press coverage and to forestall making any public announcement regarding the committee's lack of support of its party's chosen candidate.

Bryan, of course, was eager to meet with Hinkley, even in such a remote location. For New York State held 36 electoral votes, the largest amount at the time of any state in the Union. And Bryan needed to take New York to win the election. Thus, although the long trip up to Winnisook Lake would consume precious campaigning time, Bryan, nonetheless, accepted Hinkley's invitation; for he had no choice.

The day and night Bryan and his wife, Mary, spent at Winnisook was festive, the response cordial. Yet, unmoved by Bryan's famous eloquence and his undoubted charm, Hinkley remained noncommittal. And thus, opposed by James Dutcher and evaded by Major Hinkley and his committee, Bryan and his wife left the Catskills empty-handed, obtaining no firm

Lake Winnisook.

commitment or definite support. In November, the voters cast their ballots, and William McKinley, who had campaigned exclusively from his front porch—a common practice at the time—defeated Bryan by 600,000 popular and 95 electoral votes.

And so, one of the most famous men in America at the time came to the Southern Catskills and was rejected. Undaunted, Bryan, nonetheless, ran for the presidency two more times. In both 1900 and 1908, however, the results would be the same. In neither of these elections—nor in that of 1896, for that matter—would Bryan carry New York. Such are the perils of campaigning in the wilds of this state.

Interestingly, although one must recognize their differing political affiliations, James Dutcher and William Jennings Bryan, in many ways, were alike. Both were rugged individualists. Both were leaders of women and men. And both liked the limelight and found themselves the center of attention wherever they went. Ironically, it might have been more appropriate for Jim to have supported Bryan in 1896, rather than McKinley. For Bryan's policies more accurately reflected the actual interests of the inhabitants of the Southern Catskills, who had suffered greatly during the nineteenth century, due to unemployment and falling prices for farm produce, as one long depression followed another—most notably, in 1837, 1857, 1873, and 1893. The effects of this last depression, in fact, were still evident when Bryan visited the Catskills. Also, not only was Bryan a man of spirit and passion, as was Jim, Bryan was also rural, small town, and agrarian in sympathy, advocating a platform which promoted policies intended to limit the depredations of unrestrained industrialism on the common person. Throughout his career, Bryan supported public ownership of utilities, the arbitration of labor disputes, the recognition of unions, and the right to strike. He also advocated the regulation of the stock market, the protection of farmers and small merchants from the usury of banks, as well as the insurance of bank deposits by the government.[2]

Granting the existence in American politics of the frequent misapprehension of one's own best interest, Jim's quixotic conduct during Bryan's visit, nonetheless, may be explained by an event which took place some years earlier. In this instance, too, politics were evident.

The date was 1886, and, as in 1896, another prominent citizen was to visit the Southern Catskills. This person's name was Townsend Cox, and he was one of three state forest commissioners, who had been recently appointed by Governor David B. Hill. On June 11, it was planned that Cox and other dignitaries would climb to the summit of Slide Mountain and celebrate officially the establishment of the New York State Forest Preserve. Clearly, the natural guide for this trip up the mountain was Jim Dutcher, whose name was intimately associated with Slide Mountain. Jim, however, was a Republican, and Cox and the members of his party were working Democrats, all deeply interested in participating in an important public event, which would receive extensive press coverage. And so, Jim, who had blazed the trail up the mountain and had maintained it for years, was "passed over in favor of. . .C. C. Winne," an influential, local Democrat and hotelier "with a large and devoted following."[3] Offended by this treatment, Jim Dutcher, the noted guide and postmaster of Slide Mountain, nevertheless, remained unflappable and undaunted. Knowing that heavy spring rains and fierce storms had decimated the trail, Jim simply kept silent and neglected to notify the Cox party of the situation. As a result, it was reported in the press that the trip up the mountain took twice as long as planned and was unusually difficult.[4] Thus, considering the fact that Jim was slighted by the Democrats at this time, it may not be surprising, after all, that Jim was so assertive in his support of Republican candidates ten years later, when William Jennings Bryan visited the area.

Be that as it may, the late 1890s saw the high-water mark of Jim's notoriety and success. In later years, as Jim aged, he experienced significant adversity, and even greater disappointment than he had known in earlier days. In the first decade of the new century, the Panther Mountain House burned down; his wife Mary died, and two of his sons, Orison and Howard, moved to Oregon and, later, to Washington State. On mountain trips in the

1890s, Jim's youngest son, Howard, had been his constant companion. Now, Jim felt increasingly alone. Finally, what ten years earlier would have seemed an impossibility occurred. Amazingly, this paragon of Catskills life and lore sold his land, packed up, and went west. Traveling to the far western edge of the North American continent to live with his son Orison, Jim left everything that he had known and loved so deeply behind. Behind him were his wife Mary, buried, it is believed, in Oliverea in the Big Indian Valley, his remaining children, married and living their own lives, the foundations of his lost house and barn, his beloved Catskill Mountains, his post-mastership, and his local fame. As a result, Jim spent the final days of his life in an unfamiliar place, far from what he had always known as home. Buried in the Odd Fellows Cemetery in Woodland, Washington, Cowlitz County, near the Columbia River, Jim died on November 24, 1913. Similar to Richard Lionel De Lisser before him, and John Burroughs afterwards, Jim had left the Catskills never to return. The brave young man, who, as a child, had left home with nothing in his pockets, hiking over the mountains to Shandaken to cut bark, had headed out, once again, into the unknown.

CHAPTER 13
Such a spectacle as to make the heart glad

IT was estimated in 1885, by which time most of the Catskill Mountain tanneries had closed and a substantial acreage of previously barked lands had entered into the newly established Catskill Forest Preserve, that much of the original forest had been cut.[1] Yet, this was not all. The streams had been polluted, the soil depleted. And many of the animals, which had once roamed the Catskills, were gone. Believing that they would always enjoy plenty—or, more likely, not thinking at all—men drove herds of white-tailed deer into deep snow and shot every one—bucks, does, and fawns. They caught hundreds of trout, day after day, year after year, wasting most of them. They tracked down and shot the last wolf, the last elk, and finally in the early years of the twentieth century, the last mountain lion in the Catskills was killed.

Passenger pigeons nesting in the Big Indian Valley and on the East and West Branches of the Upper Neversink, in an area covering some 18 square miles—two miles wide by nine miles long—were shotgunned, netted, their necks wrung, or were clubbed to death. The local place-name of Pigeon Brook commemorates the annual nesting of passenger pigeons in this area. Taken to New York City in boatloads, they were sold in 1805 for 1¢ a bird.

It is reported that, when the great flocks of passenger pigeons, which

John James Audubon (above) and James Fenimore Cooper wrote movingly about passenger pigeons.

migrated at this time, passed overhead, they were so extensive that they obscured the sun. Meriwether Lewis of the Lewis and Clark expedition to the Pacific, while descending the Ohio River in 1803, noted this fact. And in 1813, the naturalist and artist, John James Audubon, observed and described a flock of passenger pigeons, which he estimated to include over one billion birds. Of the total bird population of the United States at the time, some 40 percent were passenger pigeons, ornithologists estimate. "The noise they made," wrote Audubon, "reminded me of a gale at sea. . . . The pigeons, arriving by thousands, alighted everywhere, one above another, until solid masses as large as hogsheads were formed on branches. . . . Here and there the perches gave way under the weight," and hundreds of birds fell to their death. "In 1805," Audubon concludes, "I saw schooners loaded in bulk with Pigeons caught up the Hudson River, coming in to the wharf at New York. . . ."[2]

Similarly, the Scottish ornithologist, Alexander Wilson, who came to America in 1794, was to write: "one charming afternoon. . .while talking with people within doors, I was suddenly struck with astonishment at a loud rushing roar, succeeded by instant darkness. . . . The people observing my surprise, coolly said, 'It is only the Pigeons'."[3] At another time during the first decade of the nineteenth century, Wilson was to compare the flight of passenger pigeons to a great celestial river, calling it a "living torrent." One flock, Wilson estimated, was 240 miles long and more than a mile wide. It contained, he calculated, over two billion birds. These pigeons, he reckoned, would consume over 17 million bushels of nuts and acorns a day.[4]

Approximately a century later, John Burroughs was to remember seeing such an awe-inspiring sight as a young person in the Catskills. In *Field and Study*, published in 1919, Burroughs was to write: "In my boyhood. . .passenger pigeons were one of the most notable spring tokens. Often late in March, or early in April, the naked backwoods would suddenly become blue with them. . .or all day the sky would be streaked with the long lines or dense masses of the moving armies." Burroughs continues, "I have seen the fields and woods fairly inundated for a day or two with those fluttering, piping, blue-and-white hosts. The very air at times seemed suddenly to turn into pigeons."[5]

At the head of Big Indian and Neversink Valleys, hundreds of thousands of passenger pigeons nested in spring. Where the state trail ascends Slide Mountain, just southwest of Winnisook Lake, the air would have been filled with chittering birds, the ground covered with guano, as if it had snowed, and broken branches and the dead bodies of birds would have been spread everywhere. The din and the stench would have been fantastic. Flocks of this beautiful blue-gray bird—the males sporting crimson breasts—distant relatives of the Rock Dove or ubiquitous urban pigeon, would have swirled overhead, forming a huge moving funnel like a great tornado.

Hungrily awaiting the arrival of these flocks would have been the local inhabitants, seeking entertainment as well as food. They would have been accompanied by the market hunters, or pigeoneers. John Burroughs describes this latter group as, "human sharks."[6] "Wild pigeons," Burroughs was to write in 1868, "in immense numbers, used to breed regularly in the valley of the Big Ingin and about the head of the Neversink." "But the gunners," he continues, "soon got wind of it, and from far and near" poured in "to slaughter both old and young."[7]

On the day following the arrival of the flocks, before daylight, boys armed with sticks knocked down and clubbed every sleeping bird they could reach. Sometimes, the very trees in which the pigeons thickly roosted were cut down, or grass fires were set beneath them, panicking the birds, which often flew into the flames and were consumed. At dawn, the shooting began, with hunters, using heavy gauge shotguns loaded with fine shot. Pointing their big guns at an angle and shooting up into the trees, each shot could kill as many as 100 of these closely-packed birds. Everyone became "wild with the pigeon-fever," wrote a contemporary observer.[8]

Only the choicest birds, however, were kept. And afterwards, the hogs of local farmers were turned loose to feed on the carcasses which had been left, the number often amounting to thousands of birds. In *The Pioneers*, published in 1823, James Fenimore Cooper, the distinguished early American writer from Cooperstown, who, at times, would set scenes from his novels in the Catskills, was to describe a similar hunt, depicting in graphic detail the carnage and the waste. In disgust, his protagonist, Leatherstocking, states, "It's much better to kill such as you want, without. . .firing into God's creatures in this wicked manner." "I don't relish to see these wasty ways. . . ."[9]

At other times, migrating pigeons were tricked into landing in traps baited with salt and grain. There, a pigeon would be tethered, its eyes blinded or sewn shut. This creature, unwittingly, would act as a decoy, attracting the wild pigeons by its movement and call. As a result, the generally unsuspicious passenger pigeons would settle to the ground and become caught, when the net was sprung. It is reported that as many as 1,500 pigeons might be taken in this fashion at one time.[10]

Sometime in the 1870s, the last great hunts of the passenger pigeon took place. And although a few pigeons were caught near Bridal Veil Falls in the present Upper Basin of the Ashokan Reservoir as late as the 1880s, they were taken in no great numbers, and never came again.[11] In the previous decade, however, a final great flock, which had nested first in Missouri and been driven into Michigan, flew east to the Catskills and nested in the Upper Beaverkill. Even here, however, they were not safe. Pursued relentlessly by the dogged pigeoneers, they were slaughtered in prodigious numbers. As a result, "tons of the birds were sent to the New York market from this nesting place." And fifteen tons of ice were used, it is reported, in their transport.[12] J. S. Van Cleef, a resident of Poughkeepsie, New York, who had been staying at the Willowemoc Lodge nearby at the time, was never to forget this event. Years later he was to recollect, this was "the last flight of pigeons that has ever taken place in this part of the country, so far as I have any knowledge. . . ."[13]

In the twentieth century, reports of rare sightings of small flocks or little groups of passenger pigeons were made. And although infrequent, each account engendered blindly optimistic predictions concerning the species' imminent return. Many of these reports, however, were bogus, or unconfirmed. And frequently, the mourning dove was mistaken for the larger passenger pigeon.

In 1906, however, John Burroughs was to write enthusiastically that the wild pigeon is "still with us," having learned that a "large flock" of passenger pigeons had passed over Prattsville in the Northwestern Catskills in April of that year. As if to corroborate this sighting, Burroughs was to state that a passenger pigeon had been shot the previous fall, and a friend had seen two pigeons in flight near West Point "a year or so ago." On the morning of May 15, 1906, in fact, a "very large flock" had flown over Kingston, and this flock was said to be "a mile long."[14] Finally, on June 30, 1906, Burroughs was to add that additional sightings had occurred—at deBruce in the Southern Catskills, and at Port Ewen and Fishkill along the Hudson River. Most of these flocks, however, were made up of only a few birds.[15]

In previous and in subsequent years, the breeding of passenger pigeons in captivity had been attempted, but ultimately, without success. And although the general public seemed mystified by the disappearance of the passenger pigeon, ornithologists did not doubt its cause. As one highly respected authority put it, "the birds were so persistently molested that they finally lost their coherence," and "were scattered far and wide. . . mainly through constant persecution by man."[16]

The last passenger pigeon, 1914.

Although attempts were made to save the passenger pigeon during its years of decline, the few laws that were proposed to protect it were either rejected, or if passed, were not enforced. People seemed unable to believe that a being, which had existed in such great numbers, could ever become extinct. Be that as it may, the last passenger pigeon died in captivity at the Cincinnati Zoological Park on September 1, 1914. It was a 29-year-old female named Martha, who, during her last years spent at the zoo, had waited patiently for a mate. Sadly, her wait had been undertaken in vain. Yet, surprisingly, no mention of this significant event in biological history appeared at the time in the pages of any major American newspaper. However, four years after the extinction of the passenger pigeon, the Migratory Bird Treaty Act of 1918 was signed, making it unlawful to "pursue, hunt. . .kill, possess, offer for sale. . .barter. . .transport or. . .carry. . .any migratory bird. . . ." But, of course, for the passenger pigeon, it was too late.

Since the year the Pilgrims landed in Massachusetts, 33 species of birds, nine species of mammals, and six species of fish have become extinct in the United States. More than 75 other species remain endangered to this day.

On the 10th of April, 1875, John Burroughs, who was born in the Catskills and who in adulthood settled on the banks of the Hudson River in the town of Esopus, was to behold the last great flight of passenger pigeons flying up the river. "For the greater part of the day," he writes, "one could not at any moment look skyward. . .without seeing several flocks. . .of migrating birds." Unhappily, Burroughs was to add, "That spectacle was never repeated. . . . The pigeons never came back. . .their vast migrating bands disappeared. . . ." "What man," Burroughs concludes, "now in his old age who witnessed in youth that. . .migration. . .would not hail it as one of the gladdest hours of his life if he could be permitted to witness it once more? It was such a spectacle. . .as to make the heart glad."[17] Describing the last few pairs of breeding passenger pigeons, which he had discovered in the wilds of northern Michigan, Chief Pokagon, a Potawatomi Native American, stated with resignation in 1895, "If the Great Spirit in His wisdom could have created a more elegant bird in plumage, form, and movement, he never did."[18]

CHAPTER 14
Deer are rarely seen

IN SHARP CONTRAST to the sad story of the passenger pigeon stands the case of the white-tailed deer. Hunted in the Catskills to the point of near disappearance, by the 1880s, according to one local historian, swine released to forage in the mountains in summer, for the most part, had replaced deer.[1]

As Charles F. Carpenter, who inspected the Catskills in 1886 upon the request of the newly established State Forest Commission, was to report: "Deer are rarely seen and much more rarely killed." "It is fair to suppose," Carpenter concludes, "that there are not a dozen deer in this whole Catskill region."[2]

In an effort to remedy this deplorable situation, two years after the creation of the Catskill Forest Preserve, the State Legislature, in 1887, authorized the State Forest Commission to establish three deer parks in the Catskills. To this end, and after extensive study and debate, a sizeable acreage on the south side of Slide Mountain was selected as the site for the first of these proposed parks. Inspected personally by Forest Commissioner Townsend Cox in mid-August, the chosen site was situated in remote and wild lands, which the state had begun to acquire ten years earlier, at the headwaters of the West Branch of the Neversink.[3] Cox himself was familiar with the intended location of the park; for the previous year, in early June of 1886, he had climbed Slide Mountain with other dignitaries to commemorate officially the establishment of the Catskill Forest Preserve, arguably, the most important legislation affecting the Catskills to be passed by the New York State Legislature in the nineteenth century. Staying overnight in each case at nearby Winnisook Lake, Cox gave his approval of the site for this early experiment in wildlife management in the Southern Catskills.

Constructed about one-half mile south of the present-day Slide Mountain Trailhead in the town of Denning near the Shandaken-Denning line in what was known as "the Old Satterlee Lot," the park would not, however, become operational until 1889, when 45 deer, which had been herded into lakes in the Adirondacks and trapped by men in boats, were shipped to the Catskills by rail and released into a fenced enclosure of some 200 acres.[4] Named for Henry Satterlee or his family, who had owned this land, the area in which the park was located had not been settled—and only sparsely, at that—until 1871.[5] And, not until 1875, by which time a primitive road had been driven up the Big Indian Valley and over the notch to the West Branch, built by local men who were paid in 50-pound bags of wheat flour, was access to this area by wagons made practicable.[6] It was here in this wilderness, it must be remembered, that, prior to the creation of the park, passenger pigeons in such prodigious numbers had previously nested. Now, visited by John Burroughs and by other curious sightseers, who drove up to the park in buggies to see the deer, the park became a popular destination and a source of amusement for tourists and for locals alike in the last decade of the nineteenth century.

Deer Park gates, Slide Mountain.
Richard Lionel De Lisser photograph courtesy of Hope Farm Press

Big Indian mail wagon.
Richard Lionel De Lisser photograph courtesy of Hope Farm Press

Constructed at an elevation of about 2,300 feet, the park was the only one of the three proposed state deer parks to be built. Nonetheless, it seems to have set a precedent for the development of other deer parks in the Catskills in subsequent years. Among these were two parks established on the grounds of the Julius Forstmann Estate about three miles farther down the Neversink in Frost Valley, another above Dry Brook on private Furlough Lake, and a fifth along the road from Haines Falls to North Lake in the Northern Catskills.[7]

The park itself was supervised, at first, by Sheridan Satterlee. "Sher," as he was called, was a native of the Catskills and of the West Branch, as his name indicates. For his work Satterlee earned $35 a month, plus the use of a caretaker's lodge. Rarely leaving the park, his supplies were delivered to the lodge by the mailman from Big Indian three times a week. Earlier, in 1886, the mail had been delivered through this area to Claryville by Benjamin North, who, interestingly, was legally blind. Only being able to distinguish night from day, Ben, nonetheless, with cane in hand, regularly walked the long miles from Big Indian to Claryville, carrying the mail.[8]

While living at the park, Satterlee fed and protected the deer, patrolled and repaired the fences, and, it is said, was very particular about the men whom he hired to assist him. Once, he fired a man, because, as he said, the man did not keep the wood box full and ate too much.[9] Although he was a straightforward and practical sort of man, surprisingly, Satterlee did not

Lodge at the State Deer Park, Slide Mountain.
Richard Lionel De Lisser photograph courtesy of Hope Farm Press

lack a sense of humor. When ordered to dispatch a troublesome old buck in the herd, he complied without objection, stating later, "I done what I was told." Nonetheless, he could not help adding dryly, "The critter had put me outten the pen so many times I decided to even the score by eatin him." But, "he was so tough I couldn't cut the gravy."[10]

Sometime in the mid-1890s, Sheridan Satterlee left his job at the park and was replaced by Cyrus Donovan. Although no images of the colorful gamekeeper, Sheriden Satterlee, exist, a photograph of Cyrus Donovan, his successor, can be found in De Lisser's *Picturesque Ulster*. Posed in front of the lodge in 1896 with his wife and three children, Donovan stands impressively, hands on his hips. In the background can be seen the rough-hewn lodge, constructed of local timber, with its fireplace chimney, elevated front porch, and its kitchen addition.[11] In later years, Sheridan Satterlee lived at his home in the nearby Esopus Valley, cutting wood, working at boarding houses, and hunting and fishing. He died there an old man in the 1930s, during the dark years of the Great Depression.[12]

Operated between 1887 and the turn of the century, the State Deer Park on the West Branch, in its day, was not considered a great success. Although the original herd of 1889 was supplemented by additional Adirondack deer in 1893 and in 1894, it was clear to everyone concerned by 1894 that these deer were not breeding well in captivity. As a result, Col. William Fox, Superintendent of State Forests, suggested that the Catskills simply be restocked with deer, rather than continue the unsuccessful breeding program. This can be accomplished, he wrote in a report, "at comparatively small expense. Within seven years those woods can be filled so thickly. . .that everyone will applaud the wisdom of the experiment."[13] Specifically, Fox recommended that deer be imported to the Catskills, held throughout the winter, and then released the following spring. This, however, was not done, and although the legislature was to reauthorize the establishment of deer parks in the Catskills in 1900, no more deer were shipped to the Catskill Park. Finally, in July of 1895, less than 100 deer were released into the Catskills—there is some disagreement as to the exact number. And Superintendent Fox and Forest Commission President Davis witnessed the process.[14] Soon thereafter, the project was abandoned, although Cyrus Donovan remained as caretaker, until the state could decide what it would do with the property. Then, for several years, the lodge and barn at the park "stood idle." At last, about 1902, most probably influenced by the 1894 amendment to the New York State Constitution which states that forest preserve lands should remain "forever. . .wild," Forest Ranger Fred Andrews and his crew "dismantled" these structures, utilizing the wood to construct a lean-to along the road, which was used by Slide Mountain campers and hikers for nearly 30 years.[15] It is said that as late as December 1972 some of the fence which enclosed the Deer Park was still standing.[16] However, little but the New York State Department of Environmental Conservation marker, erected in 1985 to commemorate this important effort to repopulate the Catskills with white-tailed deer, now remains.

Today, the establishment of the Catskill Deer Park at Slide Mountain remains controversial. Many wildlife management experts believe that this experiment was, at worst, improper and, at best, irrelevant. In fact, the respected Forest Preserve historian, Norman Van Valkenburgh, raises this very issue, when he states, "One wonders if it was in keeping with the preservation concept of forest preserve management. . .embodied in the constitution."[17] And, as C. W. Severinghaus and C. P. Brown, New York State wildlife biologists and game research investigators, write in 1956, the area was already "being reoccupied by deer" from the south and west. "Thus those released from the Catskill Park merely served to hasten slightly the natural expansion of this population."[18] Echoing this informed view, Catskill historian Alf Evers, was to write conclusively in 1961, "An important lesson in deer management had been learned in the park at Slide Mountain."[19]

And yet, although these authorities are probably correct, one cannot help but applaud the efforts of all those involved. For, certainly, it could be argued, the spirit behind this hopeful experiment was both positive and optimistic. Although the legislators, who voted in 1885 to establish the

Catskill and Adirondack Forest Preserves and again in 1887 to create the deer parks, did so for reasons both political and economic—to protect the water supply of New York State municipalities and to perpetuate the possibility of big game hunting—clearly, the result of their actions represents a changed attitude toward the environment, in general, and towards these mountainous regions, in particular.[20] In this regard, similar in intention, if more successful than the establishment of the deer park on the Neversink, was the introduction by Seth Green of German brown trout on the very same river as the deer park the previous year of 1886. Through this experiment, hatchery-raised trout helped to restore a local fishery greatly depleted by overfishing and by the degradation of a habitat ravaged by pollution, generated by tanning, unregulated in the Catskills for years.

Seth Green, fish culturist, introduced brown trout to the Catskills in the Neversink.

Nonetheless, although the original deer, which were released in 1895, may not be the ancestors of the many deer which roam the Catskills today, somehow, one cannot help but wish that this were the case. For the actions of those legislators who, in good faith, proposed this experiment, and of the men and women who worked to carry it out, the deer park heralds the development of a point of view far different from the one which had allowed tanners to bark every hemlock and pigeoneers to slaughter the last wild passenger pigeon. Regenerative and preservationist, rather than exploitative, as in the past, this experiment on the slopes of Slide Mountain in the Southern Catskills, whether successful or not, represents the beginning of a new stewardship on the part of the state. Initiated by the same impetus which founded the forest preserves, the Catskill Deer Park stands as a thoughtful and constructive example of a newfound harmony between man and nature.

CHAPTER 15
The map of the Catskill Mountains

SUCCESSFUL IN ITS DECLARED MISSION OR NOT, the construction of a State Deer Park on the Neversink, as well as the creation of the Catskill Forest Preserve, and the publication of a new map of the Catskills, drew pronounced public attention to the Southern Catskills in the late nineteenth century. Produced after nearly two decades of painstaking work begun in the summer of 1862, Arnold Henry Guyot's "Map of the Catskill Mountains," drawn by Ernest Sandoz and published in 1879, accompanied by a guidebook written by Samuel E. Rusk, helped to generate a heightened interest in this hitherto overlooked wilderness locale. As a result, in part, of Guyot's map, tourists, who, when they learned that Slide Mountain, situated at the heart of the Southern Catskills, was the highest peak in this mountain chain, flocked in droves to the boarding houses and newly constructed hotels of this area. Facilitated by the construction of the Ulster and Delaware Railroad in the early 1870s, which carried these tourists up the Esopus Valley from the Hudson River at Kingston to Pine Hill and Highmount, this influx of visitors resembles the previous migrations of the early part of the century, when Yankee settlers from the east and tanners from the north flowed into the Southern Catskills.

Pine Hill station on the Ulster & Delaware Railroad.

The man who made this map, however, was hardly interested in promoting the Southern Catskills, although this eventuality did occur. Born in

Switzerland in 1807, almost exactly 100 years after the formation of the Hardenbergh Patent, which included the Southern Catskills in its some million and one-half acres, Guyot, himself, was a man who was interested, not in profit, but in pure knowledge. A professor and geologist, Arnold Henry Guyot had studied the movement of glaciers in the Alps, after completing his doctorate in Berlin in 1835. There he had studied with the noted geographer Karl Ritter and the world famous philosopher Georg Wilhelm Friedrich Hegel. Ultimately leaving his native Switzerland at the suggestion of his friend and fellow countryman, Jean Louis Agassiz, who had preceded Guyot to the United States and had taken a position as Professor of Zoology at Harvard University, Guyot emigrated to this country in 1848, the year in which gold was discovered in California.

Upon his arrival in Boston, Guyot was invited to deliver a series of lectures at the Lowell Institute, during the winter of that year. Based on the teachings of his mentor, Karl Ritter, who had expounded the influence of geography on human history, these lectures, delivered in French, were collected, translated, and subsequently published in 1849 as a book, entitled, *Earth and Man*. This work, as well as a textbook—one of many which Guyot was to write—called *Comparative Physical and Historical Geography*, was to become highly influential and to secure for Guyot in 1854 a professorship in Physical Geography and Geology at Princeton University, a post which he was to hold for the remainder of his life.

So great was to become the influence of Guyot and his books during his lifetime that even a figure as important in the development of American environmental thought as Henry David Thoreau was to read and to consider seriously Guyot's ideas. In "Walking," one of Thoreau's most important essays, published in *The Atlantic Monthly* in 1861, one year before Guyot first visited the Catskills, Thoreau was to paraphrase "the geographer Guyot," and to echo Guyot's own enthusiasm for the New World. "America," writes Thoreau, "is made for the man of the Old World." Clearly, Thoreau writes, a "western impulse" has influenced humanity to migrate from Asia to Europe, and finally to America.[1] Similarly, in *Earth and Man*, reiterating the old theory of the course of the empire expressed earlier in 1782 by Crevecoeur, Guyot had asked: "What continent is better adapted than the American, to respond to the wants of humanity in this phase of history?"[2] And earlier in this book, as if answering this question, as well as revealing the reasons for his own emigration to the United States, Guyot was to write, "The European, who sets foot on American ground, with the purpose of making it his country, throws aside. . .his social and political past. . .takes a fresh start, recommences a new existence."[3]

Thus, the year after his arrival in the United States, Guyot, with characteristic optimism and boundless energy, began the scientific studies of his

Arnold Henry Guyot, geographer.

newly adopted country, which would make him famous, and which he would pursue until only a few years before his death. Forthwith, he began an arduous course of study of the physical configuration of the Appalachian Mountains of the Eastern United States. Beginning in 1849 in the White Mountains of New Hampshire, which he measured and surveyed for a period of four years, Guyot continued his research in subsequent years in the Green Mountains of Vermont, the Adirondacks of New York State, in Virginia, the Carolinas and Tennessee, and finally in 1859, he began his study of the Smoky Mountains of Georgia, which Guyot discovered formed "the culminating region of the whole Appalachian system."[4]

Guided by a local mountain man named Robert Collins, whose dialect Guyot could barely understand, Guyot and Collins "traveled the entire length of the crest of the Smokies, which the Appalachian Trail now follows," and, according to one authority, "must have been the first white men to do so."[5] (Today, this famous trail traverses Mount Guyot, the second highest mountain in the Smokies.) Within two years, Guyot had mapped the Smokies, developed the first comprehensive system of a nomenclature for their principal peaks, and, in 1861, had published an article in *The American Journal of Science and Arts*, called "On the Appalachian Mountain System."

CHAPTER 16
A tireless climber

GUYOT HIMSELF has been described as a man "of medium height, lean, with deep-set brown eyes and spectacles, a scholarly, professional type."[1] Nonetheless, although a scholar and already deep into middle age—he was 52 years old in 1859—Guyot was a "tireless climber" and a mountain man in his own right.[2] Having grown up in the Alps, hiking and climbing from an early age, Guyot was familiar with the outdoors, and thus, was not deterred by the rigors of wilderness travel. In fact, it is said that he enjoyed it, "building the morning fire, brewing tea, and cutting boughs for beds at nightfall."[3] However, although an enthusiastic outdoorsman and experienced Alpine traveler, Guyot found the mountains of the Eastern United States more difficult than he would have thought. For one thing, in the years prior to the American Civil War, they were, for the most part, wild and pathless. The "obstacles," Guyot wrote, "which the explorer meets in. . .wild regions," are "often very great."[4] Referring to the Appalachians, which his researches proved were one continuous mountain chain, Guyot was to write: "A chain of thirteen hundred miles in length is a vast field, especially when it includes mountains covered with interminable forests, where a footpath rarely guides the traveler's steps, and which it is impossible to cross except with a hatchet in the hand. . . ." Often, he wrote, "the journey is to be made in an unknown region. . .far from a human dwelling. . .the explorer. . .exposed to the inclement temperature of the elevated regions. . . ." "In these circumstances the danger of perishing from exhaustion is by no means imaginary, as I know by experience."[5]

But at last, Guyot came to the Catskills. It was the summer of 1862. And, having completed his work on the Southern Appalachians the previous year, and being unable to travel freely in the South due to the onset of the Civil War, Guyot cast his eyes on what, all along, had been most near. Only a bit more than 100 miles from Princeton, New Jersey, where Guyot taught, the Catskill Mountains of southern New York State, at the time, were clearly convenient to him. Long a subject of interest to this eminent geographer, and the capstone section of his masterwork on the Appalachian Mountain Chain, the Catskills had awaited Guyot for more than a decade. It was as if, somehow, he had saved the best for last.

The Catskills, of course, had been surveyed many times before Guyot's visit. In fact, they had been surveyed a number of times even before Guyot's birth. Henry Wooster of Connecticut had surveyed the Catskills for the first time in 1741. He had done this at the request of Robert Livingston, who had recently purchased an interest in the Hardenbergh Patent. Wooster's survey, however, had been partial and inconclusive. And so, eight years later, Ebeneezer Wooster had been sent to continue and to complete the work of his unsuccessful brother. Ebeneezer surveyed the Patent, in his turn, dividing its lands into 42 sections, or Great Lots, and producing a map of sorts in 1749. During this second survey, Wooster had been forced to use subterfuge to survive the wrath of local Native Americans who waylaid Wooster and his crew along the upper reaches of the East Branch of the Delaware River. Angrily, they had accused him of surveying non-Patent, Indian land. In defense, Wooster had lied to the outraged Indians, telling them that he had not been surveying their land, as it had seemed. For, as they could plainly see, his surveying chain was rusty, and, thus, unusable, having previously been immersed in the river.[6]

Other early surveyors were to follow the Wooster brothers into the Southern Catskills during the late eighteenth century. Notable among these individuals was William Cockburn, the quintessential land agent and surveyor for the Hardenbergh patentees, especially for Chancellor Robert Livingston. During the later part of the century, Cockburn, without a doubt, was the most active participant in the extensive subdivision of the Hardenbergh Patent. His maps, the first drawn in 1765, remain not only important historical documents, but also beautiful and imaginative works of art.[7] Also of note is Abraham Vernoy, who, in 1798, separated the newly formed town of Neversink from the previously existing town of Rochester, surveying these lands in the Southern Catskills and, between them, drawing the line.[8]

And so, armed with his trusty, French, Fortin mercurial barometer, and accompanied by his loyal assistants, Guyot, after 1862, and especially in the 1870s, entered each summer the mountain fastness of the Catskills, which, he admitted, he found even more daunting than other mountain ranges which he had studied. It was "an unbroken forest," he writes, with "no physical map. . .deserving the name" in existence.[9] In particular, Guyot found the Southern Catskills "pathless." This "primitive forest," he wrote, made "access anything but an easy task."[10] So dense was the undergrowth that Guyot and his crew were, at times, forced to take their measurements on mountain summits from the very tops of trees.

With Guyot, traveled a staff of able and dedicated assistants. Some, such as Ernest Sandoz, Guyot's nephew, had worked with him earlier in the Southern Appalachians. And Guyot had referred to Sandoz and the others on these expeditions with affection, calling them "my young friends."[11] In his survey of the Catskills, in addition to Sandoz, who worked primarily in the Northern Catskills, Guyot employed the services of John Reid and Samuel E. Rusk in the Eastern Catskills, William Libbey in the Southern Catskills, as well as Henry Kimball, whom Guyot called the "most indefatigable and skillful" mountain climber in the Catskills.[12]

Guyot's survey soon discovered that the formation of the Catskills was "curious," in that, although they were clearly a part of the Appalachian Chain, the Catskills ran in an opposite direction. They are an "anomaly," wrote Guyot.[13] And, regarding the Southern Catskills, in particular, he added, there is "considerable irregularity" to their physical structure.[14]

Nearly 55 years old in the summer of 1862, when he first entered the Catskills, by 1865 when he climbed and measured Black Dome Mountain in the Northern Catskills, Guyot was no longer a young man. At the time, Guyot believed that Black Dome was the Catskills' highest peak, measuring some 4003 feet, according to Guyot's calculations. But in August of 1871, guided by Henry Kimball, Guyot measured Hunter Mountain farther to the south, and proclaimed its primacy. *It* stood, he announced, at 4038 feet. At last, he had found the highest summit in the Catskills, or so he thought.

Kimball, who had begun his own explorations of the Catskills in 1847, clearly impressed Guyot with his prowess on the Hunter Mountain ascent. A somewhat self-serving individual, however, Kimball was not reluctant to celebrate his own abilities. In an article, which he wrote and published subsequently in the *Brooklyn Eagle*, Kimball was to brag unblushingly of his own hiking accomplishments. In addition, in this article, not only did Kimball assert a number of glaring inaccuracies concerning the Catskills, but he also wrote disparagingly about his employer and colleague, Arnold Guyot.[15]

Nonetheless, it was Guyot himself, at age 65, who finally entered the Southern Catskills, ascended Slide Mountain in 1872, and, ultimately, proclaimed Slide the highest in the Catskills. Describing this mountain as "quite remarkable," Guyot was to give Slide Mountain the honorific, which no one could forget. Uncharacteristically expansive, in this instance, Guyot called Slide Mountain, the "king of the Catskills."[16]

CHAPTER 17
Fitting appellations

AND SO, in the late 1870s, Guyot completed his great survey, publishing his "Map of the Catskill Mountains" in 1879 and his scientific report "On the Physical Structure and Hypsometry of the Catskill Mountain Region" in 1880 in the *American Journal of Science*. As his findings now indicate, Guyot, during his 17-year study of the Catskills, had accomplished a great deal. Not only had he produced the first accurate map of the Catskills, he had, also, determined the altitudes of peaks previously unnamed, and had corrected the altitudes of others, which had been measured inaccurately in the past. In addition, he had divided the Catskills into two major regions, separated by the Esopus Creek, and had established the fact that, not only were the Catskills a part of the Appalachian Mountain Chain, they were, also, more extensive than had been thought. In this regard, Guyot's studies found that the so-called "Shandaken Mountains," situated in Ulster County to the south of the Catskill Mountain House, were, in fact, a part of the Catskills. And Slide Mountain, in these Southern Catskills, and not Round Top, situated near the Catskill Mountain House in the Northern Catskills, as Mountain House proprietor Charles L. Beach had proclaimed, was the highest Catskill peak. This discovery not only altered the way in which the Catskills would be perceived, but also impacted the tourist business, as well as the scientific study of the Catskills, in subsequent years.

Guyot, also, had endeavored to codify the names of prominent Catskill peaks. Earlier in 1861, in his study of the Appalachian Chain, where he had first created such a nomenclature, Guyot had stated that many Appalachian peaks, due to their "uniformity of physical configuration," were unnamed. Those that *were* named, he discovered, held names of three different kinds. They were Indian names, descriptive names, or the names of human beings. As a result, Guyot developed a criteria, or "principles," which he used to name, and, in some instances, to re-name these mountains. In this regard, he was to give "preference to the name employed in the immediate neighborhood of the point designated." When more than one name had been given to the same peak, however, he adopted the name, which appeared "most natural or. . .euphonic." And when choosing between the name of a person or a descriptive characteristic, Guyot gave precedence to description, stating that in naming hitherto unnamed mountains, he "almost always preferred a descriptive name. . . ." This practice, which Guyot first developed in the Southern Appalachians, he was to apply, with some flexibility, to the Catskills. Nonetheless, Guyot was realistic in his naming, stating that "the invention of names is a thankless. . .task," for "popular usage" will decide, "in the last resort," which name is "universally adopted."[1]

Considering Guyot's sober-mindedness regarding the naming of mountains, it is interesting to note, however, how many Catskill peaks Guyot did name. In fairness to Guyot, it must be mentioned that his action may be attributed to the fact, as Guyot wrote in his 1880 scientific article that "most. . .peaks measured were. . .without names." And, therefore, he "had to find some fitting appellations." Nonetheless, the list of new names and of names changed is impressive. For example, in the Northern Catskills, Guyot named previously unnamed peaks for his assistants Samuel Rusk and Henry Kimball. (Mt. Kimball has since been renamed in honor of the painter Thomas Cole.) Guyot, also, named the peaks between Overlook and Hunter Mountains. These peaks, from east to west, Guyot called Plaaterkill, Indian Head, the Schoharie Peaks (today's Twin Mountain), Mink (Sugar Loaf Mountain), and Stony Mountain (Plateau Mountain).

Guyot, also, renamed certain mountain peaks in the Southern Catskills. He changed the name of Round Top—a common name in the Catskills—to Doubletop, South Mountain to Graham Mountain, and Dry Brook Mountain to Haynes Mountain, the latter two mountains now named for early settlers in this region.[2] It was even suggested to Guyot that he rename Hunter Mountain Mount Guyot and Slide Mountain Lion Head, or Lincoln Mountain, but Guyot declined the compliment and, in regard to Slide, refused to employ what he called "fanciful names."[3]

These examples—only a select few—suggest not only the scientific, but also the imaginative contribution which Guyot's work has made to our knowledge and understanding of the Catskills. Nonetheless, it is true, as his recent critics have indicated, that Guyot's map is not perfect; it contains errors. Some mountains are misnamed, or the names transposed on his map. A few names are misspelled, or use variant spellings. And, of course, the elevations of mountains have been found inexact by our more precise, modern methods of measurement. The 1903 U. S. G. S. map, and subsequent government topographical maps, make this evident. Even some of the names which Guyot chose with such care were changed within a decade or two after the publication of his map. Guyot's Blue Bell Mountain, for example—one of the more poetic Guyot names—has become today's North Dome.[4] And what may be considered most significant, in 1907, when the American Geographical Society released its new map of the Catskills, with an accompanying scholarly article, although Guyot's friend and colleague, Jean Louis Agassiz, who first encouraged Guyot to come to America, is mentioned, no reference can be found to the name of Arnold Henry Guyot, or to his groundbreaking map.[5]

But such revision and change are inevitable. And, of course, as a scientist and seeker of knowledge, Guyot would have known and anticipated this fact. Nonetheless, at a National Academy of Sciences meeting honoring Guyot and his lifework, Professor James D. Dana of Yale University was to remark that Guyot "made more numerous and more accurate barometric measurements than anyone else before or during his time."[6] Through his expansion of what had been known as the Catskills, and through his placement of these mountains within the great Appalachian Chain, Guyot created the Catskills, as we know them today. Clearly, his map and report stand as a Genesis of sorts, a beginning document, or even work of art, if you will, whose unified vision is engendered through the imaginativeness of his naming, and the range of his conception of place.

Recognized, also, for his work as a science educator, for his efforts on behalf of the meteorological department of the Smithsonian Institution, as well as for his Appalachian survey, Guyot's name has been given to a number of architectural and geological features. The most interesting of these is the geological term, "guyot," used to describe a flat-topped, sub-ocean mountain. Clearly, it would seem, Guyot's name has not been forgotten, and he has been appropriately and indelibly linked with mountains.

And so, after spending nearly one-quarter of his life studying the Catskills, nearly one-half of the total time he lived in the United States, Guyot returned to Princeton in the fall of 1879, where he died some four and one-half years later. So productive, however, had been Guyot as a scientist and scholar that, even after his death, hitherto unknown manuscripts were still being found. One, some 86 pages in length, was discovered in the archives of the United States Coast and Geodetic Survey. It was subsequently edited and published in 1929 as "Notes on Geography of the Mountain District of Western North Carolina," and is still considered a "major contribution" to southern Appalachian geography.[7]

In December 1883, some six weeks before his death, Guyot was to write a letter to the president of the Society of Natural Sciences in his hometown of Neuchâtel, Switzerland. In this letter, he expressed, characteristically, not only the deep love he had felt throughout his life for mountains, but also his sadness and resignation regarding his declining powers and health. Guyot writes, "Even last year I could have told you of my seventy-six years and my ability to climb our mountains, but unhappily it is not so now."[8]

CHAPTER 18
A city unto itself

IT WAS A HIKERS' HOTEL, or so it was characterized by the many journalists who enthusiastically promoted this famous hostelry. Built by a group of investors, among them Ulster and Delaware Railroad president Thomas Cornell, the Grand Hotel, constructed high up on the side of Monka Hill above Pine Hill in the Southern Catskills, opened in the summer of 1881, just a few days before its nearest competitor, the Kaaterskill Hotel, and less than 24 hours prior to the assassination of the twentieth president of the United States, James A. Garfield.[1] Arnold Guyot, the most famous Catskill Mountain hiker of the time, who had tramped the Catskills for nearly two decades and had published his influential map two years earlier, became a greatly admired guest at the Grand.[2]

Originally intended to be called the Summit Mountain Hotel, the Grand Hotel, as it was ultimately named, not only provided its guests with the most luxurious and modern of facilities available at the time, it also offered them unbounded, vigorous outdoor activity and the promise of the healthiest of natural environments. Possessing the famous Diamond Spring on site, whose crystal clear water flowed into a marble fountain constructed under a rotunda inside the entrance to the hotel, the Grand served fresh spring water to each of its 450 bedrooms every morning, the absolute purity of this beverage being celebrated throughout the Catskills. Situated nearly 40 miles from the Hudson River, with purer air and a lower population density, the Grand Hotel could boast, in addition to a most healthful environment, an unobstructed view to the southwest of Slide Mountain, the highest peak in the Catskills. This incomparable prospect, it was said, excelled all other vistas; for it was, for the most part, unsettled wilderness,

The Grand Hotel, Highmount, straddled the Ulster and Delaware county line.
Courtesy of the Delaware County Historical Association

revealing little, if any, evidence of the blemishes of industrial civilization evident from the porchs of its competitors. Thus, with the attention Guyot's map focused on Slide Mountain and the Southern Catskills, aided by a culture of the outdoors, which developed in America after the Civil War, by the railroad, which had reached the area below the hotel in 1871, and by the creation of the Catskill Forest Preserve in 1885, it is not surprising that the Grand Hotel, during the 1880s, quickly became one of the most widely praised and popular of hotels.

Variously described as "cavernous," and as "a city unto itself," the Grand Hotel was one of the largest and "most modern equipped" hotels of the time. This "large and imposing" structure, with a frontage almost 700 feet in length, straddled the Ulster-Delaware county line.[3] So big was this building that, it is said, the bar could be moved from one county to the other, as local liquor laws changed.[4] In addition to seemingly countless rooms with running water and private baths, telegraph and post office, a pharmacy with a resident physician, a grill and rathskeller, bowling alley, croquet grounds, swimming pool, tennis courts, and a nine-hole golf course with a clubhouse, the Grand Hotel also provided, for the enjoyment of its guests, a symphony orchestra, directed by Louis J. Cornu, which performed at concerts and tea dances, called "tea-dansant."[5] Charging rates starting at $31 dollars a week—three times the price of the most expensive smaller hotels

Thomas Cornell, railroad and steamboat magnate, builder of the Grand Hotel.

in nearby Pine Hill—the Grand Hotel, managed by W. F. Paige in 1883, and after 1884 by Civil War veteran Edward A. Gillett, who moved to the Grand from the Kaaterskill Hotel, the Grand maintained the highest of standards throughout its history of more than 80 years. Publicizing the purity of its air and water and the wildness of its view, the Grand Hotel, nonetheless, was a large, modern, and expensive hotel, catering in the 1880s to an affluent and socially prominent clientele. Most assuredly, therefore, at the Grand, not only nature, but also the concerns of comfort, culture, and class, were, by no means, overlooked.

One of three Catskill Mountain "railroad hotels," so-called, built accessible to railroad stations (others include the Tremper House in Phoenicia and the Overlook Mountain House above Wood-stock), the Grand Hotel was serviced by the Ulster and Delaware Railroad, which added extra trains on Friday nights to accommodate the many husbands returning from a week of work in New York. These "special" trains reached Summit Station about 10:00 P.M., and were met by a large and enthusiastic crowd of people. Reunited husbands and wives were, then, driven up to the Grand Hotel above the station in fringed coaches drawn by "showy" horses. Approaching the hotel in the darkness, the happy couples could see the long piazza of the great ark of the hotel flooded in bright, colored lights.[6] Whenever there was heavy traffic, as on Fridays, "helper" locomotives were employed to aid in the 1,100 foot climb from Phoenicia to Summit Station and the Grand Hotel. Encountering the infamous double "Horseshoe Curve" on the trip up from Pine Hill to Summit Station, new guests were surprised to find the ascent so steep that it took the train nearly two miles to rise only about 200 feet in elevation.[7]

Designed by the noted architect, John A. Wood, and built in less than one year at an initial cost of some $100,000, the Grand Hotel helped to develop Pine Hill and the surrounding area. As a result of its construction, many boarding houses and smaller hotels sprang up. Pre-existing inns, such as the Colonial Inn and the Mountain Inn, the Grand's predecessors, were expanded. And a considerable number of "handsome" private, summer residences were erected. Soon, with its Crystal Spring Bottling Works, its large summer tourist population, and its "park-like appearance," Pine Hill began to call itself, with some credibility, the "Saratoga of the Catskills."[8]

Copying the Queen Anne style of the Oriental Hotel on Coney Island, with four "projecting," Victorian mansard towers, each flying flags attached to tall poles, the Grand Hotel has been called by architectural historians, an "elegant and palatial work of art."[9] In addition to the towers, which contained bedrooms, the Grand Hotel held three floors. The second and third floors, primarily, were reserved for bedrooms. However, the first floor, although it also contained a few sleeping rooms, consisted, for the most part, of the public spaces where guests entered the hotel, mingled, and took their meals. Here, one could find the famous Rotunda and marble fountain, the parlor, breakfast room, and the commodious dining room, adorned with beautifully carved woodwork, which occupied the right, or east, wing of the hotel, and faced Slide Mountain and the unsurpassed prospect of the Southern Catskills. "Guests enter the building from the rear," it was written in 1881, "and, passing across the spacious Rotunda, gain access to the broad and lengthy piazza. . . where the wonderful mountain and valley view bursts upon them with astonishment."[10] Above the hotel, some 300 feet higher up on top of Monka Hill, one could sit in rustic lookouts, picnic, and enjoy the view. Below the hotel, one could stroll on bluestone terraces, with interconnecting stairways lined with boxes filled with brightly colored flowers, or one could descend to the tennis courts and to the swimming pool.[11]

The man who created this "palatial work of art," was born in the town of Bethel, Sullivan County, New York, in 1837. In 1863, during the height of the Civil War, he began practice in Poughkeepsie, moving his office to New York City in 1871. During the late 1860s and 1870s, according to one authority, John A. Wood was "the leading architect in the Mid-Hudson region," designing "several of Kingston's" and the region's "most prominent buildings."[12]

In Kingston, among others, Wood designed the Opera House, the Ulster Savings Bank on Wall Street, the Fitch Brothers bluestone office on the Rondout, the Kingston City Alms House on Flatbush Avenue, the Children's Church in Ponckhockie, the Loughran House and Stuyvesant Hotel on Fair Street, the Cornell Carriage House, and the New York State Armory on Broadway, as well as redesigning St. Joseph's Roman Catholic Church on the corner of Wall and Main Streets. In 1878, Wood designed the second Overlook Mountain House; in 1879, the Tremper House in Phoenicia, where on opening day a speech was delivered by the most famous minister of the

John A. Wood, architect of the Grand Hotel, converted an armory in Kingston, New York, into Saint Joseph's Church and School, 1869.

time, Henry Ward Beecher, and in 1880-1881, Wood designed what Catskill historians like to consider his masterwork—the Grand Hotel.

In later years, Wood continued his prolific career, developing plans for residential, commercial, and public buildings throughout the East, as well as in the South and Cuba. Most notable was his design of the Tampa Bay Hotel in Florida, now part of the University of Tampa campus and a National Landmark Building. Although continuing to be listed in the *New York City Directory* as an architect, Wood seems to have retired about the turn of the century, designing no new buildings after 1898. He died in Middletown, New York, on December 18, 1910, and is buried in the Evergreen Cemetery, within view of the Southern Catskills, in the town in which he was born.

CHAPTER 19
A purer, more wholesome place

A number of interesting and prominent people stayed at the Grand Hotel, although presidents and famous entertainers, actively courted by the Grand, seemed to prefer the Kaaterskill Hotel. Former President Ulysses S.

Grant, for example stayed at the Kaaterskill, as did President Chester A. Arthur, using it briefly in 1884 as his "Summer White House." And, earlier, in 1882, Oscar Wilde had lectured at the Kaaterskill, and not the Grand. Possibly, this avoidance on the part of certain individuals occurred, because the Grand Hotel was more conventional in its response to religious observance. On Sundays, formal services were conducted in the hotel, and noted clerics delivered lengthy sermons, punctuated, if not alleviated, by plentiful references to nature and to the mountains. In contrast, at the Kaaterskill, a decidedly more secular and worldly hotel, no such services were held.

For the most part, guests at the Grand Hotel were Protestant ministers and educators, accompanied by their families and wives. Jay Gould, the financier, called by the *New York Times* "the most hated man in America," preferred the Grand to the Kaaterskill, and accepted the conventional Protestant religious practices and pieties of the time. And Arnold Guyot, a guest at the Grand, although a scientist, was deeply and traditionally religious, never fully comfortable with the evolutionary ideas of Charles Darwin, as was the case, undoubtedly, with most of the guests at the Grand. Guyot's last book, in fact, was written on the subject of Christian theology.

A typical guest of the Grand, at the time, was the Reverend Theodore L. Cuyler. Cuyler had frequented the Catskill Mountain House before the construction of the Grand, and had published in the 1860s an article entitled, "A Sabbath On the Catskills." In this, somewhat, florid and sentimental essay, he described the manner in which Sundays were spent at the Catskill Mountain House. Beginning with a description of the awed and solemn observation of sunrise, followed by quiet strolls in the forest, and attendance at three religious services held throughout the day, the "parlors" of the hotel "filled by a quiet, reverential audience," Cuyler extolled the benefits of a stay at this old and venerable Northern Catskill hotel.[1] In the 1880s, however, Cuyler abandoned the Catskill Mountain House and withdrew his earlier allegiance to this hotel, when he moved to the Grand. Enthusiastically praising this newer, more modern hotel, Cuyler wrote in a subsequent article, first printed in the New York *Evangelist*, that the Grand was the superior hotel, because it had been constructed in "The Heart of the Catskills," at the "core" of the mountains, and was, therefore, a purer more wholesome place.[2]

Of course, not everyone that stayed at the Grand, or was drawn to the area by the hotel, were clerics, educators, or even pious Christians. Supreme Court Justice William Strong, who had been appointed by President Ulysses S. Grant, for example, was a guest at the Grand. After gazing off to the southwest from the Grand's great piazza, Strong was heard to remark, "I have seen the Catskills from the Hudson River. . .but this view. . .is the finest of all.[3] Other notable personages built "cottages," or purchased summer homes from early Catskill Mountain developer, J. Glentworth Butler. Italian opera singer, Amelita Galli-Curci, constructed an impressive house in High-mount above Pine Hill near the Grand, as did the noted Shakespearean actress, Julia Marlowe. The sculptor and physician, Dr. Alexander Skene, and the celebrated vocal teacher, Isadore Luckstone, also, joined this distin-guished Highmount summer community. Professor Luckstone conducted master classes there, drawing many gifted students and their parents from far and near. So renowned became this area for its artistic connections that one resident, Clara Haynes, who had spent her entire life in the area, proud-ly stated in reminiscence, "This was. . .a decided music center."[4] In this regard, in an article entitled, "Pine Hill As A Summer Resort," Catskill Mountain guidebook author, Walton Van Loan, was to write that the area is "quite picturesquely placed. . .its various structures. . .mainly new and tasteful. . .as within the past few years. . .it has come. . .to the front as a sum-mer resting place." "Few" localities "equal this [one] in all desirable ele-ments for. . .health or pleasure. . . ."[5] And later that same year, the local newspaper, the Pine Hill *Sentinel*, was to report, "Pine Hill is at the present time the liveliest town along the U & D."[6] The area even possessed an exclu-sive school and camp for Jewish boys, called the Weingart Institute, con-ducted by Dr. Samuel Weingart, which, in later years, was transformed into a country club.

Nonetheless, whether a person was a cleric or an educator, a Christian or a Jew, traditionally religious or not, during this era, a hike up Slide Moun-tain was a popular activity and a major attraction in Pine Hill and at the Grand. No able-bodied visitor to this area would have considered his or her vacation complete, if it had not included a hike up this famous mountain. To this end, stages left Big Indian regularly, taking hikers, in surprisingly large numbers, to the foot of this majestic mountain each year.[7] Thus, as Slide Mountain, the highest peak in the Catskills, attracted countless visitors to the Southern Catskills, so, too, did the Grand and other local boarding houses and hotels feed a steady stream of eager hikers to this noted moun-tain.

One such person was Dr. Howard Crosby. A friend of Rev. Cuyler, Cros-by was to praise the Southern Catskills and the Grand Hotel, as, earlier, had his colleague Cuyler. An ardent hiker and a regular guest at the Grand, Crosby was to write in the Grand Hotel's 1887 promotional booklet that the Grand was "surrounded by a wilderness of peaks," manifesting singular "grandeur and beauty."[8] A man who had been frail and ill during the early years of his life, Crosby had healed himself through vigorous, outdoor activ-ity, much as had a future president of the United States, Theodore Roosevelt. So convinced was Crosby of its healthfulness, accepting wholeheartedly the view that hiking would "do all that the best medicines can do. . .and much that they never can accomplish," Crosby had climbed every mountain peak "within a dozen miles" of the Grand, according to Rev. Cuyler. "There is not a single mountain. . .whose summit," Cuyler wrote, Crosby's "bootheels are not familiar with."[9] Becoming a sort of celebrity-climber at the Grand, Crosby was also a minister in an elite Presbyterian church in New York City, a biblical scholar, an author, and a professor of Greek. So great was his renown as a local hiker that a tower, or "observatory," on top of Belleayre Mountain, across the valley from the Grand, was given his name.

An inveterate Catskill Mountain hiker himself, the journalist Charles F. Wingate was to give social acceptability to the views of Crosby and others, regarding the salubriousness of mountain excursions. In the fashionable magazine, *Country Life in America*, Wingate was to write that "Mountain climbing is far more interesting than plain walking. . . . You follow a trail through the woods over swamps and up ledges, where. . .there is a certain spice of danger. . . ." Thus, the appropriate apparel for such adventuring, Wingate suggests, is "a sweater and moderate-weight coat; light underwear, which can be washed in any brook. . .a felt hat or cap with a brim to shade the eyes; knickerbockers" and a "few spikes in the heels" of one's shoes. "For women," Wingate asserts, "equestrian tights and Dennin [*sic*] skirts can be recommended." Reflecting not only the change in dress of women at this time, but also their increasing emancipation and consequent participation in more physically challenging activities, such as mountain climbing, Wingate points out that "It is a fixed rule that [women] shall not be helped by. . .men. When they come to a tough place they crawl or slide. . .their clothes are made for climbing."[10] In this regard, on a hike up Wittenberg Mountain near Slide Mountain, a young woman from Pittsburgh, according to a member of the hiking party, "displayed an unusual amount of endurance in climbing. . . ." "Having carried all the way a gun weighing nine pounds, besides some other articles," the woman's "determination to succeed in anything she undertakes" was made evident to her clearly impressed male companion.[11] Not surprisingly, in view of the changed attitude and lifestyle of the contemporary woman, Charles Wingate was to conclude in his own article that "A party of both sexes is always more congenial."[12]

Chapter 20
Where the works of man dwindle

OF COURSE, Slide Mountain had been climbed years before the construction of the Grand Hotel and the arrival of the fashionable and affluent in Pine Hill. The Dutchers had built the Panther Mountain House near the base of Slide Mountain about a decade earlier, and Jim Dutcher—quite famous by 1881—had already blazed a trail up the mountain, built steps in difficult sections, and had constructed a rude, wooden tower on the summit to which he guided eager boarders each summer. Local hunters, too, no doubt, had climbed the mountain before this—even, it can be suggested, before the mountain was given its present name. But when Guyot's climb of 1872 established that Slide was the highest mountain in the Catskills and his map of 1879 had publicized this fact, enthusiastic outdoorsmen and women of all sorts had flocked to the Southern Catskills, inexorably drawn to this massive mountain.

The most notable of these climbers, although, by far, not the first to ascend, or to become associated with this mountain, was John Burroughs. A fisherman and avid outdoorsman throughout his long life, John Burroughs first began to take trips into the wilderness of the Southern Catskills before the Civil War. In the summer of 1860, for example, as a young and unknown schoolteacher, as yet unpublished, Burroughs had hiked up the Beaverkill and fished and camped at Balsam Lake. Eight years later, after studying medicine briefly and meeting Ralph Waldo Emerson and Walt Whitman, Burroughs, again, entered the area of the Beaverkill, this time by way of Millbrook, crossing a mountain ridge, and ultimately reaching Alder and Thomas' (now Beecher) Lakes. This adventure Burroughs subsequently described in his essay, "Birch Browsings," collected some years later in his first book of nature essays, *Wake-Robin*.

The following June, in 1869, Burroughs, now 32 years of age, returned to the Southern Catskills. On a fishing trip to the Neversink and the Beaverkill, Burroughs not only camped and fished, but also experienced the voracious insect life and incessant rainfall of the Catskills in early summer. Sharing these delights and tribulations with an increasingly devoted readership, Burroughs wrote about this trip in his memorable essay, "Speckled Trout," which was collected, ten years later, in *Locusts and Wild Honey*.

Resigning from a position with the Treasury Department in Washington, D.C., and returning to the Hudson Valley in the same year in which Guyot climbed Slide Mountain, Burroughs became a bank examiner and farmer, purchasing land and building a house along the Hudson River in West Park.

Then, in late August of 1876, once again, drawn by the siren call of the Southern Catskill wilds, Burroughs hiked up Watson Hollow from West Shokan to Peekamoose and the headwaters of the Rondout Creek. After fishing this stream, which he described as the clearest he had ever seen, Burroughs wrote: "One is never prepared for the clearness of the water. . . . It is always a surprise." So clear, in fact, was the Rondout that it "was almost as transparent as the air. . . ." In fact, it was "like liquid air. . . ." "If I were a trout," Burroughs concludes, "I should ascend every stream till I found the Rondout."[1]

After camping and fishing this wild and lovely creek, Burroughs ascended a shoulder of Peekamoose Mountain, crossed the col, or pass, between it and Lone Mountain, and descended

Jennie Kerr, Pleasant Valley Hotel, Watson Hollow.
Courtesy of the Olive Free Library
Historical Collection

into the East Branch of the Neversink River. Here, too, he fished, spent the night in the abandoned shanty of a shinglemaker, and, finally, hiked up the West Branch of the Neversink and down to the railroad station at Big Indian. Along the way, Burroughs met the isolated settlers, mentioned earlier, who lived in this underdeveloped and desolate area. This trip was described in Burroughs' essay, "A Bed of Boughs," also collected in *Locusts and Wild Honey*.

Nonetheless, no matter how interesting and enjoyable these fishing trips were to Burroughs and to his readers, they were but a prelude and a preparation for his great ascent of Slide Mountain. And so, in August of 1884, only six months after the death of Arnold Henry Guyot, Burroughs mounted his first Slide Mountain expedition. Attempting the ascent from the east, from the area of today's West Shokan, Burroughs, "after a long and desperate climb," found himself on the summit of Wittenberg Mountain, one of Slide's neighbors, referred to in the previous chapter. The view from the summit of The Wittenberg of the Shokan Plain, which in 30 years would be flooded by the City of New York to create the Ashokan Reservoir, was "striking," admits Burroughs. But it was not Slide Mountain. And so, Burroughs salut-ed Slide from the top of a tree and "promised to call next time."[2]

Inspired by Guyot's "Map of the Catskill Mountains," which had been published just five years earlier, as well as by the chance discovery of a young, amateur botanist and ornithologist from Riverdale, New York, named Eugene P. Bicknell, Burroughs had eagerly anticipated a climb up Slide Mountain for a number of years. As he confesses in "The Heart of the Southern Catskills," an essay published in *The Century* magazine in 1888, the mountain had challenged him "for many years." "Whenever I had caught a glimpse of its summit," he wrote, "I had promised myself to set foot there before another season should pass. But the seasons came and went, and my feet got no nimbler, and Slide Mountain no lower. . . ."[3]

Deciding to climb Slide this time from Woodland Valley on the north, and accompanied by three comrades, Burroughs made this longer and more difficult ascent in early June of 1885. "We broke camp early in the morning," Burroughs writes, "and with our blankets strapped to our backs and rations in our pockets for two days set out along an ancient. . .bark road. . . ." After some confusion regarding the directions which they had been given, and after a strenuous climb, they ultimately reached the saddle, or col, between Cornell and Slide Mountains. From here, Burroughs writes, the summit of Slide "rose like a huge, rock-bound fortress. . . ." Then, the final pitch to the top was attempted, "ledge upon ledge, precipice upon precipice up which and over which we made our way slowly and with great labor, now pulling ourselves up by our hands, then cautiously finding niches for our feet and zigzagging right and left from shelf to shelf." It was "not unlike climbing a tree," Burroughs writes. Finally, after some seven hours of hiking, the party reached Slide's 4,180 foot summit, and Burroughs reports, "the fight was about all out of the best of us."[4]

Once on the summit, which was covered with a thick forest of balsam fir, Burroughs observed how less advanced was the season, due to the altitude of the mountain. "I had never before stood amid blooming claytonia, a flower of April, and looked down upon a field that held ripening strawber-ries," remarks the surprised climber. After describing the weather, which was quixotic and severe, with fog, rain, thunder clouds, and snow, Bur-roughs relates, in some detail, the domestic arrangements and the misad-ventures of the party in this high mountain wilderness. Water, food, and fuel are scarce, and cold invades the campsite at night, as do the local fauna, especially the ubiquitous porcupine.

Yet, it is the view, or "show," as Burroughs calls it, which most securely holds his attention. Marveling at the great panorama seen from atop a wooden tower erected by Jim Dutcher, Burroughs observes, "We saw the world as the hawk or the balloonist sees it. . . . How soft and flowing all the outlines of the hills and mountains beneath us. . . !" Employing the new names recently given to these mountains by Guyot, Burroughs points out Graham and Doubletop among the many other mountain peaks which can be seen from Slide's summit.[5]

And then, something amazing happens—clearly, the acme of this trip, although the account is buried in the early pages of the essay. Deeply moved by the "wild" and "aboriginal" prospect spread out before him, Burroughs experiences what might be called a personal epiphany. Awestruck, he relates, "All was mountain and forest on every hand. . . ." At this moment, Burroughs, the son of an Old School Baptist, is reminded of the fact that in the Bible mountains are presented as "holy" and "sacred." And thus, "with a feeling of surprise," Burroughs recognizes that "the great thing" is not human civilization, as we are taught, but "the earth itself. . . ." Here, therefore, Burroughs acknowledges, with humility and with reverence, that, clearly, on the summit of Slide Mountain, in the heart of the Catskills, "The works of man dwindle."[6]

CHAPTER 21
Its song was different

OF ALL THE ANIMALS which John Burroughs studied and loved, he has been most frequently associated with birds. A gifted and self-taught ornithologist, Burroughs' early passion for avian life was rekindled, when, as a young schoolteacher, he discovered in the library of the U. S. Military Academy at West Point the books of John James Audubon. It is not surprising, therefore, that when Burroughs learned of the discovery of a new species of thrush, thought to nest only on Slide Mountain, he was eager to make an ascent, hoping to observe for himself this illusive, little bird.

Discovered in 1881 by a young amateur botanist and ornithologist from Riverdale, New York, named Eugene P. Bicknell, Bicknell's thrush, as it became known, initially, was considered to be a sub-species of the grey-cheeked thrush. And, as Burroughs had written in his journal on May 27, 1865, the grey-cheeked thrush had been a "mystery" to him; for he had "never heard" its voice.[1] Not until 1995, however, more than 100 years after Bicknell's discovery, was it determined conclusively, through the application of DNA analysis, that Bicknell's Thrush was, in fact, a species in itself. Now called *Catharus bicknelli*, this thrush nests in the high country of the Northeastern United States, the Catskills forming the southernmost extent of its breeding range.

Bicknell's Thrush.

Be that as it may, on his first trip to the Catskills, from June 6 to 15, 1880, Bicknell made his "head-quarters" in Pine Hill, as he writes in his "A Review of the Summer Birds of a Part of the Catskill Mountains."[2] However, on the second and most important of his three trips to the Southern Catskills, undertaken between 1880 and 1882, Bicknell took lodgings in the Big Indian Valley, in order to be closer to Slide Mountain. Led by a local guide—possibly Jim Dutcher, since Bicknell mentions and quotes the famous Slide Mountain figure in his "Review"—Bicknell ascended Slide Mountain on June 15, 1881.[3] Interestingly, this trip occurred exactly one year after Guyot published his scholarly article, "On the Physical Geography and Hypsometry of the Catskill Mountain Region," and less than a month before the opening of the Grand Hotel.

Preceded into the Catskills by his brothers, who had collected the nests and eggs of birds there in the early 1870s, Bicknell carried with him Guyot's "Map of the Catskill Mountains," as he climbed what he called, "this comparatively unknown mountain," only "recently. . .ascertained" by Guyot "to exceed in height all other peaks of the Catskill group."[4]

It had rained during the early stages of the ascent, and it was overcast and humid, when the two men finally reached the summit. As Bicknell describes the wild scene, a "sharp wind" blew through the drenched forest and sighed "among the balsams," which were "blasted and weather beaten." To this 21-year-old naturalist raised in the outskirts of a great urban center, the mountain appeared lonely, remote, and desolate. The ground was rocky and covered with moss, and the sky overhead appeared "grey and cheerless." Even the blue jays, writes Bicknell, "seemed more subdued than in less primitive regions. . . ." Then a thrush "darted across" the trail, and disappeared into the balsams. Almost immediately, it began to sing. And Bicknell, without hesitation, realized that its "song was different." "It seemed. . .more uniform. . . with less variation and definition. . . . More subdued in tone" than other thrushes, Bicknell was to write in his everpresent "note-book."[5] Although Bicknell would obtain two specimens of this small, pale brown bird—a "new form," as he called it—and would, subsequently, seek confirmation from Robert Ridgway of the United States National Museum whether it might be a new species, Bicknell and his guide, it seems apparent, were confident, on this damp, grey day, that they had made a discovery quite momentous.[6]

Making camp on the summit, afterwards, Bicknell was to describe, in glowing terms, the beauty and the enchantment of the place. "Night was rapidly falling," he writes, "and the valleys were in darkness. . . ." Soon, a northwest wind came up, and it became cold and clear. A bright moon rose above the mountain, and by dawn on June 16, the temperature had dropped to 32 degrees. Excited and unable to sleep, Bicknell, who had just made the most important discovery of his life, stood in the darkness on a "boulder of conglomerate" rock, "on the dim mountain's brow listening for the awakening of the birds." "The increasing light upon the mountains," he observes, seems "to attract the birds from below." "Perhaps," he speculates, "they had retired [there] for the night. . . ." "Many different notes" were "to be heard about the camp. . . ." The "very isolation," he states, endows "their voices with. . .interest and charm."[7]

An exacting and respected scientist, if informally trained, slight in build, with a calm, reserved demeanor, "modest and retiring," "low voiced and quiet," Eugene Pintard Bicknell was the scion of affluent, colonial New England ancestors. Working as a banker and marrying late in life, as a young man, it is said, Bicknell possessed acute hearing. This ability, undoubtedly, aided him in his study of bird life. Although not enjoying the most "robust health," Bicknell was an "indefatigable walker," and his ability "to identify a live bird in the field" was "remarkable." Noted for maintaining detailed and meticulous records of his observations throughout his life, his lists of daily bird sightings, his notebooks, and his diaries were kept "with great faithfulness and care. . . ."

The author of some 100 publications—26 on birds and 74 on botanical subjects—Bicknell published his first article, "Evidences of the Carolinian Fauna in the Lower Hudson Valley," at the age of 18. Three years later, while climbing Slide Mountain, as mentioned earlier, he discovered the thrush which would be given his name, an honor which brought Bicknell a measure of regard and limited fame. The following year of 1882, Bicknell published "A Review of the Summer Birds of a Part of the Catskill Mountains," based on his three Catskill expeditions. This work has been considered by some authorities to be "by far the best ornithological study of the Catskill Region that has ever been printed." Publishing his first botanical papers the year prior to his Slide Mountain discovery, Bicknell, in subsequent years, also, "discovered and described" a number of new species of plants. Continuing this botanical emphasis throughout his middle years, in later life, Bicknell returned to the "pursuits of his youth," studying the birds of the Long Island shore, where he, then, lived. During these final, halcyon years, in the infancy of the twentieth century, Bicknell studied and published articles on a number of species, among them the Arcadian chickadee, the Cape May warbler, the short-eared owl, and in January, 1924—one year before his death in his 66th year—the black garfalcon.[8]

However, when John Burroughs first learned about Bicknell's discovery on Slide Mountain, Eugene Bicknell was still a very young man, relatively unknown, with the greater portion of his work ahead of him. Nonetheless, Bicknell had sent a copy of his subsequent review of Catskill Mountain birds to Burroughs, after its publication in 1882. And in this article, Bicknell had referred to Burroughs' contribution to the knowledge of ornithology as "some beautiful pen-pictures. . . ."[9] Offended by this reference, Burroughs, who was some 22 years older than Bicknell and the author of six books, among them, *Birds and Poets*, did not acknowledge receipt of the article for some time. When, finally, he did respond, Burroughs was qualified in his praise, and not uncritical. Although he admits that he read Bicknell's review "with much interest," stating it is "a very thorough timely price of work," he regrets that Bicknell has been "re-baptising some of our familiar birds in that muddy fount of scientific nomenclature, or else following the lead" of someone else. Burroughs would have preferred the new thrush to be called the Slide Mountain thrush, he declares, and not *Hylocichla Aliclae Bicknelli*, as it had been named. Admitting his antipathy to the use of scientific terminology in ornithology—and, one might add, to the naming of birds after their discoverers—Burroughs, the literary naturalist, informs Bicknell, the scientist, in no uncertain terms, that he does not "sympathize at all with this practice. It is worse than useless." "The aim of science," he states, unequivocally, "should be to simplify things. . .but ornithology of late years seems bent on making the surface confusion worse. . . . The common names of birds are alone permanent and reliable, the so-called scientific are in perpetual tilt and mutation." Concluding, Burroughs thanks Bicknell for sending him his "treatise," but adds, as if in recognition of the severity of his response, "I do not expect that you will take this spleen of mine to heart, but that is the way I feel about it."[10]

Nonetheless, granting the impassioned nature of Burroughs' reaction to Bicknell's article, and his strong reservations regarding Bicknell's scientific methodology, Burroughs is enchanted with the new thrush, when he first hears it on Slide Mountain. Immediately, he "knew" it was "a new bird, a new thrush." Describing its melodious song, Burroughs writes that the bird sounded as if it were "blowing a delicate, slender, golden tube, so fine and yet so flute-like and resonant the song appeared. At times it was like a musical whisper of great sweetness and power." "Never," he adds, "did there go up from the top of a great mountain a smaller song to greet the day. . . ." "It was but the soft hum of the balsams, interpreted and embodied" in the voice of a bird.[11]

Nearly ten years later, Burroughs remained excited about this encounter. In "Talks With Young Observers," collected in 1894 in *Riverby*, Burroughs was to write that, "One April several of those rare thrushes. . .stopped for two days" in his "current-patch" along the Hudson River. "I heard their song," he writes, "a fine, elusive strain unlike that of any other thrush." "There is a hush and privacy about its song that makes it unique," he writes. And, then, he adds wistfully, as if remembering the days he had spent earlier on Slide Mountain, "It is a bird of remote. . .mountain-tops. . . ."[12]

CHAPTER 22
The whole universe to myself

THE MOUNTAIN, which Eugene Bicknell and John Burroughs climbed in the 1880s had been part of the original Hardenbergh Patent of 1708, referred to earlier in this book. Between 1741 and 1742, Gulian Verplanck and Robert Livingston of Clermont, the second son of Robert, the first proprietor of Livingston Manor in today's Dutchess and Columbia Counties, had purchased the shares of original patentees William Nottingham, Peter Fauconnier, and Augustine Graham. Previous to these transactions, Robert Livingston himself, in 1740, had bought out the interest of May Bickley, conveyed to Bickley in 1709 by original patentee, Philip Rokeby. Thus, after the second survey of the patent in 1749 by Ebeneezer Wooster, and its division into 42 Great Lots, Verplanck and Livingston became the owners of a substantial portion of the Catskills—a total of nearly 750,000 acres, in fact. Within this vast acreage could be found Great Lot #7, in which most of Slide Mountain was situated. Through a subsequent exchange of conveyances, the northern portion of Great Lot #7 was taken by Livingston, and the southern by Verplanck.[1]

By the mid-nineteenth century, however, the area around Slide Mountain had been resurveyed and much of it sold by the heirs of Verplanck and Livingston. Referred to at the time as the "Robert L. Livingston Tract," this wilderness land had been inherited by Robert L. Livingston in 1813, through his wife, Margaret Maria, upon the death of her father, Robert R. Livingston, the "Chancellor." Robert R., who had served as Minister to France under President Thomas Jefferson, had been the grandson of Robert of Clermont, who had first involved the Livingston family, more than 70 years earlier, in the ownership of the Hardenbergh Patent.

In contrast to the Chancellor, Robert L. Livingston was "an amiable, easygoing gentleman of cultivated tastes and sensibilities" who preferred home life to the public arena. Fond of his library and the pleasures of reading the classics, Robert L. possessed little "talent for proprietorship" and finance. Finding himself "on the verge of ruin," after the stock market crash of 1837, by the time of his death in 1843, "there was little to dispose of in his will." By that time, most of his Catskills property had been sold for two dollars an acre, and the ownership of Slide Mountain had slipped through his fingers.[2]

In subsequent years, between 1877 and 1885, when the Catskill Forest Preserve was created, a substantial portion of Slide Mountain was acquired by the state through tax sales. And by 1900, through purchase from the heirs of John Kiersted, most of Slide had entered the Forest Preserve. However, it was not until 1928 that the entire Slide Mountain massif, excluding lands owned by the Winnisook Club, became public land, when a final 20-acre parcel, which included the summit itself, was approved for purchase by the state.[3]

Named for a great landslide which is thought to have occurred in July 1819, Slide Mountain, with its quartz conglomerate cap some 350 feet thick, its first-growth balsam forest, and its nesting thrush, experiences the highest rainfall and deepest snows in the Catskills—averaging 75 and 118 inches respectively—and possesses an average temperature some ten degrees lower than Rondout on the Hudson River.[4] Frequently covered by clouds, Slide Mountain experiences some of the most extreme weather in the Catskills.

It was a hot and muggy day, then, on July 22, 1893, when John Burroughs climbed Slide Mountain for, what appears to be, the last time. On the previous day, he had taken the Ulster and Delaware Railroad to Big Indian, and, then, had walked to Dutcher's Panther Mountain House, where he had spent the night. In his journal, Burroughs had written, "Tramp up Big Indian valley. . .my roll of blankets on my back. . . . "[5] The next morning he began

Slide Mountain from Woodland Valley.
Courtesy of Hope Farm Press

the ascent of Slide Mountain from Winnisook Lake, stopping to drink copiously at springs along the trail. In contrast to previous trips, however, this time Burroughs climbed alone.

Although he had invited a fellow guest at Dutcher's to accompany him on the ascent—perhaps, as a matter of courtesy—on this day, Burroughs clearly preferred to climb the mountain without a companion. He was "glad," he wrote to his son, "to have the mountain all to" himself. Or, as he was to write, with obvious satisfaction, in a subsequent letter to a friend, "I passed a night alone on the summit—had the whole universe to myself."[6]

Much had changed in Burroughs' life, since, with his friend, Myron Benton, and his West Park neighbors, the VanBenschoten brothers, he had first climbed Slide and heard Bicknell's thrush. Burroughs was 56, now, and no longer a young man. His son, Julian, remembers that his father had seemed "introspective" and "alone," at the time. There had been a disagreement, or "family jar," between his mother and father, he writes. Relations between his parents had been strained for some time, it is apparent, and they would agree in the fall to live apart.[7]

By the summer of 1893, Burroughs had published nine books, with *Riverby*, which would include his essay "The Heart of the Southern Catskills," in process. In two years, he would build a rustic cabin, called "Slabsides," in the woods near his riverside home. Here, he would entertain

**John Burroughs, writer and naturalist, in his twenties
and his wife, Ursula North Burroughs.**

his many admirers, and, from spring through fall, live alone. Burroughs, too, was rapidly becoming a celebrity, and soon, he would commence his world travels, becoming the frequent guest of the rich and the influential.

Introverted and philosophical by nature, Burroughs, in the early 1890s, entered a period of extensive self-examination, taking careful stock of his life and times. Jay Gould, the infamous tycoon and so-called "Robber Baron," who had stayed at the Grand Hotel, and who had been Burroughs' childhood classmate, had just died the previous year, and this had increased Burroughs' own highly developed sense of mortality. In the spring of 1893, the country had descended into financial depression, once again, with worldwide panic ensuing. Three million men and women had become unemployed, it was estimated, and tens of thousands of tramps were roaming the countryside. In response, the newly elected president, Grover Cleveland, had called a special session of Congress, but it would not meet until late summer. The fact that Cleveland had been reelected at all, in 1892, the first Democrat to become president since James Buchanan in 1856, offered evidence of what one historian has called, a "sense of mounting crisis. . . ."[8] John Burroughs, himself, had traveled to Washington, D.C., to see Cleveland inaugurated. Burroughs had even visited his old house on V. Street, where he and his young wife had once lived. "What a host of thoughts and memories crowd in upon me," he was to write on March 3, 1893.[9] Clearly,

John Burroughs in later life and his friend, the poet Walt Whitman.

Burroughs' own situation mirrored that of the country in this period of uncertainty and confusion.

More significant to Burroughs' state of mind, at the time, however, was the death of his mentor and friend, the poet Walt Whitman, who had died on March 26, 1892. Although Whitman had been declining for some time, his death had been a "devastating blow" to Burroughs, and he had been "unhinged almost to the point of collapse," as a result.[10] Burroughs had served as an honorary pallbearer at Whitman's funeral, but had been unable to speak, when asked, so overcome was he with emotion. For days afterward, Burroughs was unable to sleep. "I am just back home from the funeral. . .and am a good deal broken up," he was to write to a friend.[11] "I thought I was prepared for Walt's departure. . .but I find I was not," he was to write to another.[12] In subsequent journal entries, Burroughs was to refer to Whitman as "Dear Master," and, finally, after some time, to assert that he was "fairly well these days, but sad, sad."[13]

Troubled by periodic bouts of depression throughout his life, Burroughs' melancholy deepened after the death of Whitman and the estrangement from his wife. In a letter written to his old friend and hiking partner, Myron Benton, during the winter before his last Slide Mountain ascent, Burroughs was to write: "The solitude of life increases. . .the shadows are a little deeper and longer. . . ." And, later, he was to declare that everyone, now, seemed so young to him. "I live in the past not the present."[14]

Eighteen years younger than Whitman, when they met in 1863 in Wash-

Above: **John Burroughs at Winnisook Club with young members.**
Courtesy of Herbert L. Shultz

Below: **John Burroughs at his summer home near Roxbury, New York.**

ington, D.C. during the Civil War, where Burroughs had worked as a clerk in the Treasury Department and Whitman had ministered to the wounded in local military hospitals, Burroughs, subsequently, invited Whitman to visit him at Riverby, his home in West Park, New York. And Whitman had done so with delight a number of times during the late 1870s. These happy occasions Whitman was to memorialize in sketches, which were subsequently published and later collected in *Specimen Days*.

Deeply influenced by Whitman's book of poems, *Leaves of Grass*, and by the person of Walt Whitman himself, Burroughs, in turn, was to spend a considerable amount of time and effort writing about Whitman and his work. From the publication of his first book, *Notes on Walt Whitman as Poet and Person*, published four years after Whitman and Burroughs met, to the inclusion of a final essay on Whitman, called "The Poet of the Cosmos," which was included in the last book which Burroughs published during his lifetime, Burroughs, throughout his life, was to promote and to celebrate enthusiastically this great American poet. In fact, between Whitman's death in 1892 and 1896, when Burroughs' *Whitman: A Study* was published, Burroughs was to write no fewer than 25 items on Whitman.[15] Declaring in *Whitman: A Study* that he had "accepted Whitman entire and without reservation," Burroughs was to claim that Whitman was "the one mountain thus far in our literary landscape."[16]

And so, mourning the death of his beloved friend and the disintegration of his marriage, lonely and alone, Burroughs ascended the mountain upon which he had found peace and gained deep insight eight years earlier. In sorrow and confusion, he sought the space and the solitude of Slide Mountain, once again. Brokenhearted, Burroughs returned to the "heart" of the Catskills, hoping to heal himself and to find solace. At this critical moment in his life, therefore, Slide Mountain, at the "heart" of the Catskills, became, in effect, the center of Burroughs' universe.

Chapter 23
The last encampment

IT WAS NEARLY 100 YEARS, since William and Ann Denman had settled on the Upper Neversink, within sight of Slide Mountain, ten miles to the northeast. Their descendants still lived on the old farm, somehow managing to scrape an existence out of the rocky soil, even in such difficult times. By 1893, the Yankees, who had migrated to the Catskills in the dawn of the century, had been absorbed into the local culture, long ago. And the tanners, for

Slide Mountain

Above: **Slide Mountain and the Burroughs Range from the site of the Grand Hotel.**
Below: Slide Mountain from Friday Mountain.
Author's photographs

the most part, had come and gone, leaving the forest depleted of hemlock, the results of their activity still evident, unused tanneries crumbling into ruins. Although few, if any, passenger pigeons nested any longer in the trees above the Slide Mountain trail, which Burroughs climbed on this last trip up Slide, a mountain lion had been killed near Dutcher's Panther Mountain House just a few years earlier.[1] And in the next year of 1894, a provision would be added to the State Constitution protecting Slide Mountain and other peaks in the Catskill Preserve, keeping them "forever. . .wild. . . ."[2]

Reaching the summit of Slide Mountain about two o'clock, Burroughs established his final encampment. Here, he built a "snug camp," or "nest," spreading out his two old Army blankets, blue-grey in color, with black stripes at each end, under the rock ledge where he had slept in 1885. "They were smoke-scented from a hundred camp fires and there were holes burned in them. . . ." The view from this spot, Burroughs was to report to his son, was "very grand," and in his journal, he was to describe it as truly "sublime."[3] That night, about seven o'clock, and lasting for about an hour, one of the great thunderstorms for which the Catskill Mountains are famous "came up." And Burroughs, "safely stowed away" beneath the summit rock, could look "straight out" and into the "thunder-cloud" from Slide's great height. With amazement, he could actually see, he wrote, "the bolts forged," and peer into its "heart of fire."[4]

No essay, however, was inspired by this awesome experience. Nor is Bicknell's thrush mentioned, as it was described with such delight in 1885. And there were no companions, or witnesses, to confirm Burroughs' emotions at the time. In his journal entries, which describe this last night spent on the summit of Slide, Burroughs is surprisingly circumspect. It is as if he has turned inward, and is examining his own interior drama, its tumultuousness reflected in the storminess of the exterior landscape—that "heart of fire." In this regard, one notices how much Burroughs chooses not to report. His journal jottings are elliptical, as if the material were too personal to share, or inappropriate for the purposes of art. In a comment, tantalizing abstract and general, Burroughs only writes in summary, "what a vivid sense of the presence of those mountains I brought back. . . ."[5]

Nonetheless, the images of light and of power—of infinity, even—presented, initially, in somewhat abbreviated form, remained with John Burroughs for some time. In fact, he was to refer to this profound experience in his correspondence for over a year with reverence and with awe. Safe in his "nest," he had looked out and into the heart of a storm, much as he had faced, honestly and forthrightly, his own emotional problems at the time. As a result, he had gained the strength and the perspective he had sought from this experience to accept and to transcend the troubling events, which were occurring in his own life and time.

With the advent of the new century, Burroughs, now in his 60s, would observe even greater changes in his life and in the Catskills than he could have thought possible that night on the summit of Slide. In the coming years, Burroughs would visit Woodland Valley at the base of Slide a number of times, camping so close, as he was to write, that he could hear the great mountain "purr."[6] But, inexorably, his popularity would become pronounced, his books be used as textbooks in classrooms across the country, and his white-bearded visage become familiar to everyone far and wide. As a result, his company would be sought avidly by prominent personages, and he would find himself far from his beloved Catskills for extended periods of time. In 1899, for example, he would travel with E. H. Harriman as his guest on an expedition to Alaska, and soon thereafter, he would accompany the young President Theodore Roosevelt to the American West.

Burroughs would spend his last summers at Woodchuck Lodge on the old, family farm near Roxbury, many miles across the Catskills from Slide. In October of 1920, during the last months of his life, a visitor to the lodge would give Burroughs a spruce tree obtained from the summit of Slide. And just prior to his final departure from the Catskills, Burroughs would plant this seedling at the site he had chosen for his burial place. Five months later, on March 29, 1921, Burroughs would die in Ohio, while traveling by rail, returning to the Catskills from California. His last words are appropriate and moving. "How far are we from home?" it is recorded, he asked.[7]

Although, John Burroughs was buried, as he had planned, near Roxbury on the old farm, the plaque affixed to his Boyhood Rock at the gravesite is not his only memorial. In 1923, two years after Burroughs' death, members of the Winnisook Club, whom Burroughs had visited at their rustic retreat on the northwestern flank of Slide, erected a memorial on the mountain's summit to John Burroughs. Its inscription reads, in part: He "introduced Slide Mountain to the world. . .made many visits to this peak and slept several nights beneath this rock. . . . In the Heart of the Southern Catskills."

EPILOGUE

AT THE TURN OF THE CENTURY, the distinguished Adirondack photographer, Seneca Ray Stoddard, visited the Southern Catskills, climbed Slide Mountain, and photographed the summit. Recognizing Slide's preeminence and its centrality to the Catskills, Stoddard, through this act of creation, linked the two mountain ranges and celebrated through his art the union of the Adirondacks and the Catskills, originally established in 1885 by the legislation which created the New York State Forest Preserve.

Reminiscent of the interest paid by the Hudson River School of painters to the Northern Catskills during the early decades of the nineteenth century, these photographs of Stoddard, and those of De Lisser taken a few years earlier, engendered an increase in the visibility of the Southern Catskills, and presaged the profound changes, which would occur in the area in the new century.

During the ensuing three decades of the twentieth century, public holdings in the Catskills were expanded substantially, and an extensive trail system built, following Jim Dutcher's legacy. State fire towers were constructed on a number of summits, the first in the Southern Catskills on Balsam Lake Mountain in 1909.[1] And, in the same year, within a little more than a decade after John Burroughs' last climb of Slide Mountain, a meeting was held in the Southern Catskills, which drastically changed the traditional way of life led in the Catskills, and even transformed the very landscape.

On August 5-7, at the Grand Hotel—only ten miles from Slide's summit—New York State Water Commissioners, in a series of private discussions held behind closed doors, planned the strategy and determined the legal steps to be taken, which would convert the Esopus Valley into the first of six New York City reservoirs to be constructed in the Catskills. This momentous meeting initiated the process whereby, over the next 60 years, most of the major waterways in the Catskills would be dammed, and their water sent to New York. When these reservoirs were completed in 1967, over 20 towns and villages were lost, some 60,000 acres inundated, nearly 6,000 inhabitants dispossessed and displaced—many of them descendants of the earliest settlers of the region—and over 10,000 graves were disinterred, the remains often taken to locations far from their original resting place.[2]

When these plans were finally made public, a shock wave spread throughout the Catskills. The noted journalist and fly fisherman, Theodore Gordon, for one, was clearly upset, although grudgingly accepting of the project. In 1905, he was to write, with resignation, "This is probably the last season for fly-fishing in the lower Esopus. . .millions of inhabitants in New York City must be supplied with pure water."[3]

The locals, of course, were overwhelmed. In 1955, in fact, after one-half a century of reservoir construction in the Catskills, Mary Jane Shaver, caught in the hopeless and, now, sadly familiar process of dispossession— this time precipitated by the construction of the Pepacton Reservoir, the 5th of six New York City reservoirs to be built—was to exclaim: "I feel like [I'm] being torn up by the roots. Every bit of earth around has memories. . . ." Jane's neighbor, Orson Slack, an old man in his 80s at the time, was to add, "I've been West and I've been South. But I kin tell you there's no place like right here in this old valley."[4]

Above: **The Esopus Valley in the 1890s, before the Ashokan Reservoir.**
Richard Lionel De Lisser photograph courtesy of Hope Farm Press

Below: **Orson Slack, one of many moved when the Pepacton Reservoir was built.**
Courtesy of Herbert Haufrecht

Norman Studer in 1977, teacher, writer, folklorist, director of Camp Woodland.
Author photograph

Norman Studer at Camp Woodland, his pioneering interracial camp near Phoenicia, 1940s.
Courtesy of Herbert Haufrecht

Norman Studer, a folklorist and Director of Camp Woodland near Phoenicia, New York, was an eyewitness to this diaspora. In a moving article published in the *New York Folklore Quarterly*, Studer describes the scene: "When the last resident moved out of the village [of Arena]…on a rainy morning in October, 1955, human history came to an end in eighteen miles of bottomlands along the East Branch of the Delaware River in the Catskills. I had seen life come to a standstill in this valley during the past ten years. In the process of building a huge reservoir, New York City moved out of this area every evidence of man's handiwork. . . . Houses were torn down, trees grubbed, bodies removed from. . .graves. We saw the surveyors come, the big earth dam rise, and the. . .villages. . .disappear one after the other. Then the waters came and. . .the land with all of its richness of human history and tradition was flattened into. . .anonymity. . . ."[5]

Beyond the rise and fall of tanning and subsequent forest products industries, the creation of the Forest Preserve, the building of hotels and boarding houses, the development of private clubs, estates, and preserves, and even the introduction of new technology, such as the railroad and the automobile, which brought the next great wave of European immigrants into the Catskills, the construction of New York City's Water System produced the most profound and pronounced change in the Catskill Mountains, since the establishment of the Hardenbergh Patent. Although census records reveal that, between 1880 and 1920, farm tenancy declined in New York State, in the Catskills, for the most part, the descendants of the original settlers remained on ancestral lands, if only producing a portion of their livelihood, at the time, through farming. Although it became impossible to compete successfully with Western farmers, due to the declining fertility of the soil and the conditions of hill farming, which made it impossible to use the new machinery on mountainsides, the inhabitants of the Catskills retained the ability to make a living, one way or the other, through hunting, fishing, and gathering, working in the forest, or the workshop, serving as game wardens, or as caretakers on private clubs and estates.

Nonetheless, with the advent of the New York City Water System in the Catskills, the "Age of Homespun," as it is called, came to an end, and a place and a way of life that had long been supported by old and tested patterns was forever lost. Within the space of one, or, at most, two generations, the Catskills' vibrant, traditional culture disappeared; the old folks and their old ways were quickly forgotten, and, not unlike a fond and fading memory, they soon became the stuff of myth and folklore. But that is another story, one which will be told in the next volume of this series.

NOTES

CHAPTER 1

1. J. H. Mather, *Geography of New York* (New York, 1847), 182. See, also, Alf
   Evers, *The Catskills: From Wilderness to Woodstock* (Garden City, New York:
   Doubleday, 1972), ft. nt. 16, 765-766.

2. Alf Evers, "The Shandaken Mountains and Asher Durand," *The Ulster County Townsman*, 5 January 1961, 2. See, also, Bob Steuding, *A Catskill Mountain
   Journal* (Fleischmanns, New York: Purple Mountain Press, 1990), 34-36.

3. Arnold Guyot, *Map of the Catskill Mountains* (New York: Scribners, 1879).

4. All quotations from the major published works of John Burroughs have been
   taken, unless otherwise indicated, from the 23-volume Riverby Edition of *The
   Writings of John Burroughs* (New York: Houghton Mifflin, published
   between 1904-1923). See *Writings*, 1: 171; 9: 37-66.

5. Michael Kudish, "Vegetational History of the Catskill High Peaks," (Ph.D.
   diss., State University College of Forestry at Syracuse University, 1971), 221;
   Nathaniel Bartlett Sylvester, *History of Ulster County, New York* (Philadelphia: Everts and Peck, 1880), 2: 292 f.; James E. Quinlan, *History of Sullivan
   County* (Liberty, New York: G. M. Beebe and W. T. Morgans, 1873), 456 f.,
   reprinted 1965.

6. Thorough discussions of the Hardenbergh Patent are to be found in: John D.
   Monroe, *Chapters in the History of Delaware County, New York* (Delhi, New
   York: Delaware County Historical Association, 1949), 13 f.; Evers, *The
   Catskills*, 28 f. The territory discussed in this history is contained, for the
   most part, in Great Lots 5-10.

7. Harry Albert Haring, *Our Catskill Mountains* (New York: G. P. Putnams,
   1931), 264 f.; Edward G. West, "The Catskills: 'Here the Works of Man Dwindle'," *The Conservationist*, October-November 1962, 7-8; Monroe, 87 f.; Joshua
   Gerow, *Alder Lake: A Symposium of Nostalgic and Natural Observation*
   (Liberty, New York: Fuelane Press, 1953), 114-115.

8. Kudish, "Vegetational History," 221.

9. A notable example of such violence occurred in the Southern Catskills at the
   Chestnut Woods at Grahamsville on September 5, 1778, when Lieutenant John
   Graham and a contingent of some 20 men were ambushed, massacred,
   scalped, and dismembered by a group of Tories and Native Americans. At this
   time, attacks on civilians were not uncommon, with raiding, abduction, and
   murder, as well as the burning of homesteads, and even the abandonment of
   some settlements, resulting.

10. D. W. Meinig, "Geography of Expansion, 1785-1855," in *Geography of New
    York State*, ed. John H. Thompson (Syracuse, New York: Syracuse University
    Press, 1966), 140.

11. Monroe, 260.

12. George Dangerfield, *Chancellor Robert R. Livingston of New York, 1746-1813*
    (New York: Harcourt, Brace, 1960), 15; Barbara Wakefield Purcell, ed., *Time*

and the Valley: Story of the Upper Rondout Valley (Town of Neversink Bicentennial Commission, 1978), 24.

13. Clare Brandt, *An American Aristocracy: The Livingstons* (Garden City, New York: Doubleday, 1986), 81.

14. Jerome Mushkat and Joseph G. Rayback, *Martin Van Buren: Law, Politics, and the Shaping of the Republican Idealogy* (Dekalb, Illinois: Northern Illinois University Press, 1997), 66. See, also, the cases cited on 210, ft. nts. 2-4.

15. Evers, *The Catskills*, 208. See also: Reeve Huston, *Land and Freedom: Rural Society, Popular Protest, and Party Politics in Antebellum New York* (New York: Oxford University Press, 2000); David Maldwyn Ellis, *Landlords and Farmers in the Hudson-Mohawk Region, 1790-1850* (Ithaca, New York: Cornell University Press, 1946), reprinted 1967; Dorothy Kubik, *A Free Soil--A Free People: The Anti-Rent War in Delaware County, New York* (Fleischmanns, New York: Purple Mountain Press, 1997). For imaginative responses to the Anti-Rent War see: Mary Bogardus, *Crisis in the Catskills* (New York: Vantage, 1960); and Henry Christman, *Tin Horns and Calico* (New York: Henry Holt, 1945).

16. Arthur S. Link, *The American People: A History*, Vol. 1 (Arlington, Illinois: AHM Publishing, 1981), 253.

17. Dale Van Every, *Ark of Empire: The American Frontier 1784-1803* (New York: William Morrow, 1963), 20 f. A fine distinction is made by historian Ted Morgan in *Wilderness at Dawn: The Settling of the North American Continent* (New York: Simon and Schuster, 1993), 14-16, between a "hinterland" and the frontier. Thus, according to Morgan, although, for the most part, unsettled in the 1780s, the Southern Catskills would be considered a hinterland, since, by that time, they lay east of the recognized line of national settlement.

18. George Brown Tindall and David E. Shi, *America: A Narrative History*, 5th ed., Vol. 1 (New York: Norton, 1999), 328-329.

CHAPTER 2

1. Ted Waddell, "Denmans Celebrate 200 Years in Neversink Valley," *Sullivan County Democrat*, August 1995. The descendants of Ann and William Denman have been generous with the assistance they have given the author. Among these individuals have been Paul Denman, James Cooper, Louise Hunter, and Dr. Thomas McGrath.

2. Link, *The American People*, 254.

3. David Hackett Fischer, *Albion's Seed: Four British Folkways in America* (New York: Oxford University Press, 1989) 207 f., 787.

4. Quinlan, *History of Sullivan County*, 464.

5. Dangerfield, *Chancellor*, 425.

6. Arnold Guyot, "On the Physical Structure and Hypsometry of the Catskill Mountain Region," *American Journal of Science* [Third Series] 19, no. 114 (June 1880): 430.

7. Sylvester, *History of Ulster County*, 2: 330.

8. T. Morris Longstreth, *The Catskills* (New York: Century, 1918), 293.

9. Kudish, "Vegetational History," 59.

10. Sylvester, 332.

11. Kudish, 15.
12. Howard Hendricks, "The Town of Hardenburgh," in *The History of Ulster County, New York*, ed. Alphonso T. Clearwater (Kingston, New York: W. J. Van Deusen, 1907), 258.
13. Timothy Dwight, "Journey to Niagara," Letter 1, *Travels in New-England and New-York*, Barbara Miller Solomon, ed. (Cambridge, Massachusetts: Belknap Press, 1969). First published (New Haven, Connecticut: Yale University Press, 1821-22).
14. Henry David Thoreau, "Ktaadn," *The Maine Woods*, in *Henry David Thoreau* (New York: The Library of America, 1985), 603. Thoreau had visited the Northern Catskills in the summer of 1844. He had viewed with delight the area around North and South Lakes. Unfortunately, Thoreau did not visit the Southern Catskills, nor did he remark on them from a distance, as had Timothy Dwight.
15. Burroughs, *Writings*, 4: 187.
16. Burroughs, 190.
17. Burroughs, 112.
18. David Freeman Hawke, *Everyday Life in Early America* (New York: Harper and Row, 1988), 3.

CHAPTER 3
1. Hawke, *Everyday Life in Early America*, 7.
2. Henry E. Dwight, "Account of the Catskill Mountains," *American Journal of Science and Arts* 2, no. 1 (1820): 28, 29.
3. Helen Lane, ed. *The Story of Walton* (Walton, New York: Walton Historical Society, 1975), 10.
4. Leah Showers Wiltse, *Pioneer Days in the Catskill High Peaks* (Hensonville, New York: Black Dome Press, 1999), 35.
5. Kudish, "Vegetational History," 31.
6. Kudish, 36-39.
7. Kudish, 44.
8. Quinlan, *History of Sullivan County*, 480-81.
9. Kenneth E. Hasbrouck, "History of the Town of Denning," in *The History of Ulster County With Emphasis Upon the Last 100 Years* (Ulster County Historical Society, 1984), 26.
10. Haring, *Our Catskill Mountains*, 29.
11. Henry Griffeth, "The Town of Shandaken," in *The History of Ulster County, New York*, ed. Alphonso T. Clearwater (Kingston, New York: W. J. Van Deusen, 1907), 368.
12. Elwood Hitchcock, *Big Hollow* (Hensonville, New York: Black Dome Press, 1993), 49-50.
13. Hitchcock, 32.
14. Purcell, *Time and the Valley*, 86-87.
15. Lena O. B. Tiffany, *Pioneers of the Beaverkill Valley* (Laurens, New York: Village Printer, 1976), 13-14; Doris West Brooks, *The Old Eagle-Nester, The Lost Legends of the Catskills* (Hensonville, New York: Black Dome Press, 1992), 25.

16. Hitchcock, 57, 81.
17. Paul Denman and James Cooper, telephone interviews by the author, 16 October 2000, 4 June 2001, 9 June 2001.

CHAPTER 4

1. Michael Kudish, *The Catskill Forest* (Fleischmanns, New York: Purple Mountain Press, 2000), 82-86.
2. Robert P. McIntosh, "Forests of the Catskill Mountains, New York," *Ecological Monographs* 42 (Spring 1972): 153. See, also,: McIntosh, "The Forest Cover of the Catskill Mountain Region, New York, as Indicated by Land Survey Records," *The American Midland Naturalist* 68 (October 1962): 416.
3. Michael Kudish, lectures delivered at Belleayre Ski Center, Highmount, New York, 29 August 1999 and at Catskill Center for Conservation and Development, Arkville, New York, 11 June 2000.
4. Paul W. Gates, *The Farmer's Age: Agriculture 1815-1860*, 2nd ed. (New York: Harper and Row, 1968): 34. Gates states that in 1821, in New York State, potash brought $121.25 per ton, nearly one million dollars per year. See, also: David M. Ellis, et. al., *A History of New York State*, revised ed., (Ithaca, New York: Cornell University Press, 1967), 163-165, 167; William Cronon, *Changes in the Land: Indians, Colonists, and the Ecology of New England* (New York: Hill and Wang, 1983), 116-117; Jared Van Wagenen, *The Golden Age of Homespun* (Ithaca, New York: Cornell University Press, 1953), 26-33.
5. Evers, *The Catskills*, 209; Hitchcock, *Big Hollow*, 56; Cronon, 116.
6. Ellis, 165.
7. Purcell, *Time and the Valley*, 32.
8. Purcell, 33.
9. Ellis, 163-165. See, also, John C. Cook, "From Farmland to Forest," *The Conservationist*, October-November 1974, 10.
10. Hawke, *Everyday Life in Early America*, 32; Kudish, "Vegetational History," 60; Quinlan, *History of Sullivan County*, 153-155.
11. Thomas S. Wermuth, *Rip Van Winkle's Neighbors: The Transformation of Rural Society in the Hudson River Valley, 1720-1850* (Albany, New York: State University of New York Press, 2001). See, also: Wermuth, "Economic Opportunity and Moral Economy in the Hudson River Valley During the American Revolution," *The Hudson River Regional Review* 14, no. 2 (September 1997): 5-23; Ellis, *Landlords*, ch. 3.
12. Hawke, 38.
13. John Burroughs, "The Apple," in *Picturesque Catskills, Greene County*, ed. Richard Lionel De Lisser (Northampton, Massachusetts: Picturesque Publishing Company, 1894), 92, reprinted (Cornwallville, New York: Hope Farm Press, 1967).
14. Ulysses Prentiss Hedrick, *The Land of the Crooked Tree* (New York: Oxford University Press, 1948), 158-159.
15. Ellis, *Landlords*, 116.
16. Burroughs, *Writings*, 7: 239-240.
17. Ernest Ingersoll, "At the Gateway of the Catskills," *Harper's New Monthly*

Magazine 54 (December 1876-May 1877): 820-821.

18. Douglas De Natle, *Two Stones For Every Dirt: The Story of Delaware County, New York* (Fleischmanns, New York: Purple Mountain Press, 1987), 88; Ruth Freeman, *The Frugal Housewife* (Watkins Glen, New York: Century House, 1957), 4.

19. Norman Studer, ed., *A Catskill Woodsman: Mike Todd's Story* (Fleischmanns, New York: Purple Mountain Press, 1988), 14-15.

20. Purcell, 30, 43.

21. Tindall, *America*, 356.

22. John Burroughs in *John Burroughs Talks: His Reminiscences and Comments*, Clifton Johnson, ed. (New York: Houghton Mifflin, 1922), 50, 51; *Writings*, 7: 233-261.

23. Purcell, 40.

CHAPTER 5

1. Allan Nevins, ed., *American Social History as Recorded by British Travellers* (New York, 1923), 33.

2. Gates, *Farmer's Age*, 31.

3. Meinig, "Geography of Expansion," 143; Ellis, *History of New York State*, 187.

4. Evers, *The Catskills*, 282; Gates, 31.

5. Dixon Ryan Fox, *Yankees and Yorkers* (New York: University Press, 1940), 18, reprinted (Ira J. Friedman, 1963).

6. Burroughs, *Writings*, 3: 183; Burroughs, *My Boyhood* (Garden City, New York: Doubleday, Page and Company, 1922), 9.

7. Hitchcock, *Big Hollow*, 8-10.

8. Sylvester, *History of Ulster County*, 326.

9. Sylvester, 293, 305-306; Quinlan, *History of Sullivan County*, 458-459, 465, 492-493; Vera Van Steenbergh Sickler, *History of the Town of Olive, 1823-1973* (privately printed, 1973), 5-6.

10. Gina Giuliano, "Eight Generations: The Eckert Family in West Shokan, 1792-1999," *Kaatskill Life* 14, no. 4 (Winter 1999-2000): 16-23.

11. Ed Van Put, *The Beaverkill* (New York: Lyons and Burford, 1996), 13-15; Quinlan, 492-493; Tiffany, *Pioneers of the Beaverkill Valley*, 5-6; Joan Powell and Irene Barnhart, *Beaverkill Valley, A Journey Through Time* (Lew Beach, New York: B. P. Publishing Company, 1999), 24; Gerow, *Alder Lake*, 14. In contrast to the previous sources, Gerow states that it is "reasonable to believe" that the first settlers from Connecticut came to the Beaverkill after 1815.

12. L. H. Butterfield, ed., *Adams Family Correspondence* (Cambridge, Massachusetts: Harvard University Press, 1963), 2: 76.

13. Washington Irving, *A History of New York*, ed. Edwin T. Bowden (New Haven, Connecticut: College and University Press, 1964), bk. 3, ch. 7, 154-158.

14. Samuel L. Clemens, *A Connecticut Yankee In King Arthur's Court* (New York: Harper and Row, 1889), 4-5.

15. Fox, 116.

16. R. R. Livingston, letter to R. Livingston, 4 June 1776, Livingston-Redmond

Papers, Franklin Delano Roosevelt Library, Hyde Park, New York.

17. Fox, 200-206.
18. Jamie O. Shafer, "A Propper Yankee in Central New York: The Diary of Mary Bishop Cushman, 1795-1797," *New York History* 79, no. 3 (July 1998): 263, 275.
19. Fox, 211-212.
20. Fox, 221.
21. Fox, 222.
22. Fox, 25, 176.
23. Fox, 192.
24. Fox, 195.

CHAPTER 6

1. William Edwards, *Memoirs of Colonel William Edwards* (Washington, D. C.: privately printed, 1897), 99.
2. David S. Rotenstein, "Tanbark Tycoons: Palen Family Sullivan County Tanneries, 1832-1871," *The Hudson Valley Regional Review* 15, no. 2 (September 1998): 1.
3. Richard Wiles, "The Tanning Industry in Greene County," *Hudson Valley Studies* (June 1983): 8.
4. Frank Norcross, *A History of the New York Swamp* (New York: Chiswick Press, 1901), 51-54.
5. Norcross, 51-54.
6. Norcross, n. p.
7. Richard Wiles, *Windham* (Saugerties, New York: Hope Farm Press, 1985), 7.
8. Evers, *The Catskills*, 385-386.
9. The main tannery building, according to Patricia Millen, *Bare Trees: Zadock Pratt, Master Tanner…* (Hensonville, New York: Black Dome Press, 1995), 13, was 530 feet long by 43 feet wide and 2-1/2 stories high. Lawrence Gardiner, "Prattsville's Master Tanner," *The Catskills* 2, no. 2 (Spring 1974): 7, says 550 feet long. See, also, Maury Klein, *The Life and Legend of Jay Gould* (Baltimore: Johns Hopkins University Press, 1986), 44.
10. Millen, 87.
11. Henry Hedges Prout, *Old Times in Windham* (Cornwallville, New York: Hope Farm Press, 1970), 49-50; Evers, 342.
12. Evers, 343.
13. Evers, 347.
14. Zadock Pratt, *Chronological Biography of the Hon. Zadock Pratt of Prattsville, N. Y.* (New York: Shoe and Leather Press, 1876), 8.
15. Klein, 44.
16. Millen, 5. Kudish, *The Catskill Forest*, 158, says one million hides.
17. Ann S. Stephens, "The Tanner and the Hemlock," *New York Illustrated News*, reprinted in *The Prattsville Advocate*, 2 June 1853; Millen, 64-67.

CHAPTER 7

1. Jay Gould, *History of Delaware County and the Border Wars of New York* (Roxbury, New York: Keeny and Gould, 1856), 11.

2. Haring, *Our Catskill Mountains*, 84.
3. R. L. Buttrick, "Woodstock's Woods and Their Effect On Its History and People," in McIntosh, "The Forest Cover," 411.
4. West, "The Catskills," 7.
5. McIntosh, 420.
6. Kudish, *The Catskill Forest*, 57.
7. Kudish, "Vegetational History," 66.
8. Millen, *Bare Trees*, 91.
9. *Report of the Forestry Commission of the State of New York* (Albany, New York, 1886). See, also, Evers, *The Catskills*, 584.
10. *Sixth Annual Report of the Forest, Fish and Game Commission of the State of New York 1900* (Albany, New York, 1901), 27.
11. A. B. Recknagel, "The Forests of the Catskills," *The Conservationist*, December 1920, 181.
12. Jack E. Hope, "The Catskill Tanning Industry—Its Rise and Fall," *The Conservationist*, October-November 1960, 28-29.
13. A. W. Hoffman, "The Passing of the Hemlock," in Richard Lionel De Lisser, *Picturesque Ulster* (Kingston, New York: Styles and Bruyn Publishing, 1896), 187.
14. Charles S. Kendeigh, "Breeding Birds of the Beech-Maple-Hemlock Community," *Ecology* 27, no. 3 (July 1946): 237.
15. Kudish, "Vegetational History," 65.
16. Ellis, *Landords*, 210, 160-163. See, also, Field Horne, *The Greene County: A History* (Hensonville, New York: Black Dome Press, 1994), 65.
17. William F. Fox, "History of the Lumber Industry in the State of New York," in *Sixth Annual Report of the Forest, Fish and Game Commission of the State of New York 1900* (Albany, New York, 1901), 62.
18. Haring, 96.
19. Norman J. Van Valkenburgh, *The Forest Preserve of New York State in the Adirondack and Catskill Mountains: A Short History*, revised edition (Fleischmanns, New York: Purple Mountain Press, 1996); Van Valkenburgh, "History of the Catskill Park and Forest Preserve," in *The Catskill Park: Inside the Blue Line*, Van Valkenburgh and Christopher W. Olney, eds. (Hensonville, New York: Black Dome Press, 2004); Evers, *The Catskills*, 581-589.

CHAPTER 8
1. Gerow, *Alder Lake*, 116.
2. Kudish, *Catskill Forest*, 58.
3. Joseph F. Willis, "Forest-Based Industries," in *The River and the Mountains: Readings in Sullivan County History*, ed. David M. Gold (South Fallsburg, New York: Marielle Press, 1994), 156.
4. Martin Bruegel, *Farm, Shop, Landing: The Rise of a Market Society in the Hudson Valley, 1780-1860* (Durham: Duke University, 2002), 81-82.
5. Kudish, *Catskill Forest*, 158; Millen, *Bare Trees*, 83-84, says a bit more.
6. Haring, *Our Catskill Mountains*, 93-95, says 3-10 trees per cord.
7. Robert P. McIntosh, *The Forests of the Catskill Mountains, New York* (Cornwal-

lville, New York: Hope Farm Press, 1977), 12; Kudish, "Vegetational History," 67.

8. Alf Evers, "The Tannery Brook," *Woodstock Times*, 10 April 1975, 13.
9. Gerow, 119.
10. Millen, 13.
11. Millen, 78-83; Gerow, 120.
12. Hope, "Catskill Tanning Industry," 28.
13. Norcross, *History of the New York Swamp*, 54.
14. Millen, 77.
15. Barbara McMartin, *Hides, Hemlocks and Adirondack History: How the Tanning Industry Influenced the Region's Growth* (Utica, New York: North Country Books, 1992), 24.
16. Norcross, 66.
17. Norcross, 91.
18. Wiltse, *Pioneer Days*, 29.
19. Millen, 16.
20. Lonnie and Ruth Gale, *Shandaken, New York: A Pictorial History* (Fleischmanns, New York: Purple Mountain Press, 1999), 21.
21. Bruegel, 139.

CHAPTER 9

1. George A. Petrides, *Trees and Shrubs* (Boston: Houghton Mifflin, 1956), 21-22.
2. Petrides, 21.
3. Kudish, *Catskill Forest*, 159-160.
4. De Lisser, *Picturesque Ulster*, 192.
5. Kudish, 159.
6. Norcross, *History of the New York Swamp*, 167 f.
7. Hoffman, "The Passing of the Hemlock," 188-189. Also retold in Haring, 91-92 and Evers, *The Catskills*, 392.
8. Kudish, 159.
9. Kudish, 159-160.
10. Kudish, 159. De Witt C. Davis, "Town of Olive," in *The History of Ulster County, New York*, ed. Alphonso T. Clearwater (Kingston, New York: W. J. Van Deusen, 1907), 325, 330; Sylvester, *History of Ulster County*, 2: 297.
11. Kudish, 111.
12. Burroughs, *Writings*, 4: 180.
13. Elwyn C. Davis, *West Shokan: The Eden of the Catskills* (West Shokan, New York: Ladies' Aid Society of the Olive-Shokan Baptist Church, 1930), 14; De Witt Davis, 330; Benjamin Turner, "Olive History Given by Turner," mimeographed copy of address given in West Shokan, New York, 4 July 1876; Kudish, 159.
14. Elwyn Davis, interviewed by the author, September 1973-January 1975.
15. De Witt Davis, 325, 330.
16. Jeff Muise, *Old Bob's Gift: Life in the Catskill Mountains of the 1850s* (Wappingers Falls, New York: Shawangunk Press, 1996), 60.
17. Haring, *Our Catskill Mountains*, 92-93; Kudish, 158; Muise, 59.

18. Haring, 92-93.
19. Sylvester, 2: 298.
20. Sylvester, 2: 302.
21. Quinlan, *History of Sullivan County*, 459; Monroe, *Chapters in the History of Delaware County*, 17; Howard Fletcher Davidson, *Delaware County: Fur Trading to Farming* (Delhi, New York: R. B. Decker Advertising, 1976), 35.
22. George Erts, "Denning History," unpublished ms. in typescript, 25 February 1975, 1.
23. Letter of William H. Denning of New York City to Richard D. Childs of Grahamsville, New York, Sullivan County, 6 April 1841. Xeroxed copy in author's collection.
24. Hamilton Child, *Gazetteer and Business Directory of Sullivan County, New York For 1872-73* (Syracuse, New York: The Journal Office, 1872), 191; Quinlan, 466; Kudish, 157.
25. Sylvester, 2: 333; Kudish, 157.
26. Purcell, *Time and the Valley*, 51-52; George B. Reynolds, "Memories of Long Ago: History of Events in Town of Neversink," published serially in the *Republican Watchman*, Monticello, New York and the *Ellenville Press*, Ellenville, New York, 1936, reprinted as a booklet.
27. Monroe H. Wright, *Along the Neversink in the Seventies* (Liberty, New York: Liberty Register, n.d.), 3.
28. De Lisser, 154-155.
29. *Brass Buttons and Leather* (Sullivan County Historical Society, 1963), 37; Gerow, *Alder Lake*, 117; Van Put, *The Beaverkill*, 46; Tiffany, *Pioneers of the Beaverkill Valley*, 61; Powell, *Beaverkill Valley*, 85; Kudish, 156.
30. Quinlan, 511-512; Child, 281; Gerow, 117; *Brass Buttons*, 42; Kudish, 157.
31. Henry Steele Commager, ed., *The Era of Reform, 1830-1860* (New York: D. Van Nostrand, 1960), 76-77.

CHAPTER 10
 1. De Lisser, *Picturesque Ulster*, 191.
 2. De Lisser, 191.
 3. De Lisser, 191.
 4. Studer, *A Catskill Woodsman*, 95.
 5. De Lisser, 155-156.
 6. Studer, 96.
 7. Millen, *Bare Trees*, 22.
 8. Millen, 22; Gerow, *Alder Lake*, 119.
 9. Gerow, 119.
10. Studer, 95.
11. De Lisser, 190.
12. Hedrick, *Land of the Crooked Tree*, 239.
13. Horace Greeley, *New-York Weekly Tribune*, 18 April 1843, 102.
14. Wiltse, *Pioneer Days*, 30.
15. Wiles, *Windham*, 15.
16. Norman Cazden, Herbert Haufrecht, and Norman Studer, eds., *Folk Songs of*

the Catskills (Albany, New York: State University of New York Press, 1982), 13.

CHAPTER 11

1. *Commemorative Biographical Record of Ulster County, New York* (Chicago: J. H. Beers, 1896), 734.
2. Kudish, "Vegetational History," 240, no. 20; *Catskill Forest*, 109.
3. De Lisser, *Picturesque Ulster*, 158.
4. De Lisser, 158.
5. De Lisser, 214, 217, 221.
6. De Lisser, 220.
7. Doris Dutcher Randall, interview by the author, 1 March 2005.
8. Arthur G. Adams, et. al., *Guide to the Catskills* (New York: Walking News, 1975), 275.
9. Alf Evers, "Foreword," in *Picturesque Ulster*, Richard Lionel De Lisser, n. p.
10. Kudish, *Catskill Forest*, 160.

CHAPTER 12

1. Herbert L. Shultz, *A Winnisook Chronicle, 1886-1986* (privately printed, 1986), 12.
2. Irving Stone, *They Also Ran* (New York: New American Library, 1968 ed., first published 1943), 84; Harold U. Faulkner and Mark Starr, *Labor in America* (New York: Harper and Brothers, 1944), 78.
3. Evers, *The Catskills*, 579.
4. *New York Times*, 12 June 1886; Kingston *Daily Freeman*, 11 June 1886; Kingston *Daily Leader*, 14 June 1886.

CHAPTER 13

1. Kudish, *Catskill Forest*, 71.
2. John James Audubon, *The Audubon Reader*, ed. Scott Russell Sanders (Bloomington, Indiana: Indiana University Press, 1986), 102-104.
3. Alexander Wilson, qtd. in *The Passenger Pigeon*, W. B. Mershorn (Deposit, New York: Outing Press, 1907), 19-20.
4. Wilson, qtd. in *Birds of America*, Part 3, Edward Howe Forbush, et. al., eds. (Garden City, New York: Garden City Publishing Company, 1936), 40.
5. Burroughs, *Writings*, 20: 3-5.
6. Burroughs, *Writings*, 3: 90.
7. Burroughs, *Writings*, 1: 174.
8. Quinlan, *History of Sullivan County*, 508.
9. James Fenimore Cooper, *The Pioneers* (New York: New American Library, 1964), 237.
10. Allan W. Eckert, *The Silent Sky: the Incredible Extinction of the Passenger Pigeon* (Dayton, Ohio: Landall Press, 1965), 82-84; Charlton Ogburn, "The Passing of the Passenger Pigeon," *American Heritage* 12 (June 1961): 33; Hedrick, "Passenger Pigeons," *Land of the Crooked Tree*, 46-60.
11. John Bierhorst, *The Ashokan Catskills: A Natural History* (Fleischmanns, New York: Purple Mountain Press, 1995), 48.
12. Forbush, *Birds of America*, 42.

13. J. S. Van Cleef, "Recollections of 'Old Times'," *Forest and Stream*, 20 May 1899, qtd. in *The Passenger Pigeon*, Mershorn, 140. See, also: William T. Brent, "Wild Pigeons," in *Picturesque Ulster*, De Lisser, 164-165; Tiffany, *Pioneers of the Beaverkill Valley*, 10, 62; Burroughs, *Writings*, 1: 174; 4: 113, 186-187, 218.
14. Burroughs, *Forest and Stream*, 19 May 1906, qtd. in Mershorn, 180-181.
15. Burroughs, qtd. in Mershorn, 183-185.
16. Forbush, 43.
17. Burroughs, *Writings*, 20: 3-5; 12: 96-97; 3: 90-91.
18. Chief Pokagon, *Chautauquan* 22, no. 20 (November 1895), qtd. in Ogburn, 91.

CHAPTER 14

1. Quinlan, *History of Sullivan County*, 507 f.
2. Charles F. Carpenter, "The Catskill Preserve," in *Second Annual Report of the Forest Commission of the State of New York* (Albany, New York, 1887), 116.
3. Michael Kudish, "Forest History of Frost Valley," *Adirondac* 49, no. 3 (April 1985): 17.
4. Regarding the size of the Catskill Deer Park, see: Alf Evers, "Slide Mountain—King of the Catskills," *The Conservationist*, June-July 1961, 6; *The Catskills*, 588; Randolph Kerr and Norman Van Valkenburgh, "Catskill Forest Preserve," *The Conservationist*, April-May 1973, 10.
5. Kudish, 17.
6. Kudish, 17; Erts, "Denning History," 5; Sylvester, *History of Ulster County, New York*, 2: 332-333.
7. Kudish, *Catskill Forest*, 154.
8. *Town of Shandaken* (Town of Shandaken Bicentennial Commission, 1976), 26.
9. Bryan E. Burgin, "The Catskill Deer Park," *The Conservationist*, April-May 1973, 44.
10. Burgin, 44.
11. De Lisser, *Picturesque Ulster*, 145, 218; Erts, 9.
12. Burgin, 44.
13. Burgin, 44.
14. Kudish, "Frost Valley," 18; *Catskill Forest*, 154; Burgin, 44; Evers, "Slide Mountain," 6; *The Catskills*, 588; Van Valkenburgh and Olney, *The Catskill Park*, 56.
15. Burgin, 44.
16. Burgin, 11.
17. Van Valkenburgh and Olney, 56.
18. Burgin, 44.
19. Evers, "Slide Mountain," 6.
20. See Carpenter, 99. See, also, Verplanck Colvin, in 24th *Annual Report on the New York State Museum of Natural History* (Albany, New York, 1870).

CHAPTER 15

1. Henry David Thoreau, *The Portable Thoreau*, Carl Bode, ed. (New York: Viking Penguin, 1982 ed.), 606.
2. Arnold Henry Guyot, *Earth and Man: Lectures on Comparative Physical Geography*, C. C. Felton, trans. (Boston: Gould and Lincoln, 4th ed. rev.,

1851), 324. J. Hector St. John de Crevecoeur, "Letter 3, What Is An American," *Letters From An American Farmer* (New York: E. P. Dutton, 1957, first published, 1782). Crevecour writes: "Americans are western pilgrims, who are carrying along with them that great mass of arts, sciences, vigor, and industry which began long since in the east; they will finish the great circle."

3. Guyot, 321-322.
4. Arnold Henry Guyot, "On the Appalachian Mountain System," *American Journal of Science and Arts* [Second Series] 31, no. 92 (March 1861): 159.
5. Charlton Ogburn, *The Southern Appalachians: A Wilderness Quest* (New York: William Morrow, 1975), 58.

CHAPTER 16

1. Michael Frome, *Strangers in High Places: The Story of the Great Smoky Mountains* (Garden City, New York: Doubleday, 1966), 95.
2. Frome, 95.
3. Frome, 95.
4. Guyot, "Appalachian Mountain System," 157.
5. Guyot, 158.
6. Evers, *The Catskills*, 62.
7. Evers, 270, 366, 389.
8. Purcell, *Time and the Valley*, 17.
9. Guyot, "Physical Structure," 429.
10. Guyot, "Physical Structure, 430, 444.
11. Guyot, "Appalachian Mountain System," 164-165.
12. Guyot, "Physical Structure," 431.
13. Richard Lionel De Lisser, *Picturesque Catskills, Greene County* (Northampton, Massachusetts: Picturesque Publishing, 1894), 92; Guyot, "Physical Structure," 430.
14. Guyot, "Physical Structure," 444.
15. Henry Kimball, "The Catskill Mountains," Kingston *Daily Freeman*, 31 August 1874, reprinted from the *Brooklyn Eagle*.
16. Guyot, "Physical Structure," 445.

CHAPTER 17

1. Guyot, "Appalachian Mountain System," 178-180.
2. Guyot, "Physical Structure," 434-435.
3. Guyot, "Physical Structure," 434.
4. Adams, *Guide to the Catskills*, 279-280.
5. Angelo Heilprin, "The Catskill Mountains," *Bulletin of the American Geographical Society* 39, no. 4 (1907): 193-201.
6. Frome, *Strangers*, 112.
7. Frome, 111.
8. Frome, 112.

CHAPTER 18

1. Disagreement exists regarding the exact date of the opening of the Grand Hotel. Gerald M. Best, *The Ulster and Delaware Railroad Through the Catskills*

(San Marino, California: Golden West Books, 1972), 39, says June 22, 1881. Alf Evers, "Parks in the Catskills," *In Catskill Country* (Woodstock, New York: Overlook Press, 1995), 111, says 1880, although, in *The Catskills*, 504, he writes that the hotel opened at "a grand. . .ball" on July 1, 1881. Adams, *Guide to the Catskills*, 251, also, cites this date, no doubt, referencing Evers. For additional information regarding Thomas Cornell, see: Bob Steuding, *Rondout: A Hudson River Port* (Fleischmanns, New York: Purple Mountain Press, 1995).

2. Adams, *Guide to the Catskills*, 251.
3. Roland Van Zandt, *The Catskill Mountain House* (New Brunswick, New Jersey: Rutgers University Press, 1966), 261; Best, 39, 69; *The Catskills, An Illustrated Hand-Book and Souvenir* (Kingston, New York: Ferris Publication Company, 1897), 100-101.
4. Evers, *The Catskills*, 507.
5. Best, 69.
6. Clara A. Haynes, "Saga of Highmount," unpublished ms. in typescript, 1949, 1.
7. *Van Loan's Catskill Mountain Guide* (New York: Dudley Press, 1914), 85; *The Catskills, An Illustrated Hand-Book*, 100; Best, 30, 135.
8. *The Catskills, An Illustrated Hand-Book*, 101.
9. *Resorts of the Catskills*, The Architectural League of New York (New York: St. Martin's Press, 1979), 26, 14.
10. *Resorts*, 17.
11. Evers, "Parks in the Catskills," 111.
12. William B. Rhoads, *Kingston, New York: The Architectural Guide* (Hensonville, New York: Black Dome Press, 2003), 179.

CHAPTER 19
1. Theodore L. Cuyler, "A Sabbath On the Catskills," in *The Catskill Mountains and the Region Around*, ed. Charles Rockwell (New York: Taintor Brothers, 1867), 261.
2. "The Heart of the Catskills" was reprinted in the promotional booklet *The New Grand Hotel, Catskill Mountains*, ed. Edward A. Gillett, 1887.
3. Best, *Ulster and Delaware Railroad*, 67.
4. Haynes, "Saga of Highmount," 2.
5. Walton Van Loan, "Pine Hill As A Summer Resort," Pine Hill *Sentinel*, 22 June 1887.
6. "Local News," Pine Hill *Sentinel*, 13 July 1887.
7. Gale, *Shandaken, New York*, 65.
8. Gillett, *The New Grand Hotel, Catskill Mountains*, 1887.
9. Gillett, *The New Grand Hotel, Catskill Mountains*, 1888; John Forbes, *The Physician's Holiday, or a Month in Switzerland in the Summer of 1848* (London, 1853), 12-13.
10. Charles F. Wingate, "Climbing the Catskills," *Country Life in America* 3 (June 1905): 220.
11. C. W. V., "On Top of The Catskills," The *Argus*, 1 September 1875.
12. Wingate, 220.

CHAPTER 20

1. Burroughs, *Writings*, 4: 166-167.
2. Burroughs, *Writings*, 9: 39-40.
3. Burroughs, *Writings*, 9: 39.
4. Burroughs, *Writings*, 9: 43, 46-47.
5. Burroughs, *Writings*, 9: 47, 57, 48. Nearly 70 mountain peaks in the Catskills, Green Mountains of Vermont, the Berkshires of Massachusetts, and in the Hudson Valley can be seen from the summit of Slide Mountain, according to Evers, "Slide Mountain—King of the Catskills," 6. See, also, Sylvester, *History of Ulster County*, 2: 310-12.
6. Burroughs, *Writings*, 9: 48, 49.

CHAPTER 21

1. John Burroughs, *The Heart of Burroughs's Journals*, Clara Barrus, ed. (Port Washington, New York: Kennikat Press, 1967), 40, originally published (New York: Houghton Mifflin, 1928).
2. Eugene P. Bicknell, "A Review of the Summer Birds of a Part of the Catskill Mountains," *Transactions of the Linnaean Society of New York* 1 (1882): 117.
3. Bicknell, "A Review," 164, 165.
4. Bicknell, "A Review," 118.
5. Eugene P. Bicknell, "A Sketch of the Home of Hylocichla Aliciae Bicknelli, Ridgway, With Some Critical Remarks on the Allies of this New Race," *Bulletin of the Nuttall Ornithological Club* 7, no. 3 (1882): 153, 155, 156.
6. Robert Ridgway, "Descriptions of Two New Thrushes From the United States," *Proceedings of the United States National Museum* 4 (1882): 374-379.
7. Bicknell, "A Sketch," 156.
8. Maunsell Schieffelin Crosby, "In Memoriam: Eugene Pintard Bicknell, 1859-1925," *The Auk: A Quarterly Journal of Ornithology* 43, no. 2 (April 1926): 143-149.
9. Bicknell, "A Review," 116.
10. John Burroughs, *The Life and Letters of John Burroughs*, Clara Barrus, ed., 2 vols. (New York: Russell and Russell, 1968), 1: 274-275, originally published (New York: Houghton Mifflin, 1925).
11. Burroughs, *Writings*, 9: 51, 53-54.
12. Burroughs, *Writings*, 9: 327-328.

CHAPTER 22

1. Monroe, *Chapters*, 17-18; Davidson, *Delaware County*, 35.
2. Sylvester, *History of Ulster County*, 2: 305; Brandt, *An American Aristocracy*, 178-181.
3. Evers, "Slide Mountain," 3-6; Kudish, *Catskill Forest*, 71-73, 108. See, also, Norman J. Van Valkenburgh, *Land Acquisition For New York State: An Historical Perspective* (Arkville, New York: Catskill Center, 1985), 20-21, 42.
4. Kudish, "Vegetational History," 36, 38, 46.
5. Burroughs, *Life and Letters*, 1: 341.
6. John Burroughs, *My Boyhood*, 167; *Life and Letters*, 1: 349.

7. Burroughs, *My Boyhood*, 166.
8. Page Smith, *The Rise of Industrial America: A People's History of the Post-Reconstruction Era*, Vol. 6 (New York: McGraw-Hill, 1984), 508, 484.
9. Burroughs, *Heart of Burroughs's Journals*, 175.
10. Perry D. Westbrook, *John Burroughs* (New York: Twayne, 1974), 39; "John Burroughs and the Transcendentalists," *Emerson Society Quarterly* No. 55, Part 2 (Second Quarter 1969): 53.
11. John Burroughs and Ludella Peck, *John Burroughs and Ludella Peck* (New York: Harold Vinal, 1925), 3.
12. Westbrook, *John Burroughs*, 39.
13. Clara Barrus, *Whitman and Burroughs Comrades* (New York: Houghton Mifflin, 1931), 298; Burroughs, *Life and Letters*, 1: 325.
14. Letters to Myron Benton, in Berg Collection, New York Public Library, 14 January 1893, 6 November 1893.
15. Westbrook, *John Burroughs*, 40.
16. Burroughs, *Writings*, 16: 297, 299.

CHAPTER 23
1. Pine Hill *Sentinel*, 1 December 1886.
2. Article 14 of the New York State Constitution. See, also, Evers, *The Catskills*, 587.
3. Burroughs, *My Boyhood*, 167, 168; *Life and Letters*, 1: 341.
4. Burroughs, *My Boyhood*, 167; *Life and Letters*, 1: 341, 349.
5. Burroughs, *Life and Letters*, 1: 342.
6. Burroughs, *Life and Letters*, 2: 78.
7. Edward J. Renehan, *John Burroughs: An American Naturalist* (Post Mills, Vermont: Chelsea Green, 1992), 313.

EPILOGUE
1. Martin Podskoch, *Fire Towers of the Catskills: Their History and Lore* (Fleischmanns, New York: Purple Mountain Press, 2000), 30.
2. Diane Galusha, *Liquid Assets: A History of New York City's Water System* (Fleischmanns, New York: Purple Mountain Press, 1999), 268, 270-271.
3. Bonnie Marranca, ed., *A Hudson Valley Reader* (Woodstock, New York: Overlook Press, 1991), 287.
4. Norman Studer, "Folklore From A Valley That Died," *New York Folklore Quarterly* 12, no. 3 (Autumn 1956): 193.
5. Studer, 192.

BIBLIOGRAPHY

Ackerly, Loretta. *Township of Neversink, 1798-1998.* Privately printed, 1998.

Adams, Arthur G. *The Catskills: A Guide to the Mountains and Nearby Valleys.* Fleischmanns, New York: Purple Mountain Press, 1988.

_____. *Guide to the Catskills.* New York: Walking News, 1975.

Addison, Richard. "The Catskills." *Harper's New Monthly Magazine* 9, no. 50 (July 1854): 145-158.

Alexander, E. J. "An Unsought Adventure in the Southern Catskills." *Journal of the New York Botanical Garden* 37 (1936): 42-46.

Aley, Laura. *The Valley—Facts and Legends on Big Indian and Oliverea.* Big Indian, New York: Oliverea Fire Department Auxiliary, 1973.

Audubon, John James. *The Audubon Reader.* Scott Russell Sanders, ed. Bloomington, Indiana: Indiana University Press, 1986.

Bailyn, Bernard. *Voyages to the West: A Passage in the Peopling of America on the Eve of the Revolution.* New York: Alfred Knopf, 1986.

Balsam Lake Mountain Wild Forest Unit Management Plan. New Paltz, New York: New York State Department of Environmental Conservation, revised January 1996.

Barrus, Clara. *Whitman and Burroughs Comrades.* New York: Houghton Mifflin, 1931, reprinted Port Washington, New York: Kennikat Press, 1968.

Bartlett, Irving H. *The American Mind in the Mid-Nineteenth Century.* New York: Thomas Y. Crowell, 1967.

Becker, William. *The Ulster County Directory.* No. 1. Kingston, New York, 1907.

Beers, Frederick W. *County Atlas of Ulster, New York.* New York: Walker and Jewett, 1875.

Benincasa, Janis, ed. *I Walked the Road Again: Great Stories From the Catskill Mountains.* Fleischmanns, New York: Purple Mountain Press, 1994.

Bennet, John and Seth Masia. *Walks in the Catskills.* New York: East Woods Press, 1974.

Best, Gerald M. *The Ulster and Delaware Railroad Through the Catskills.* San Marino, California: Golden West Books, 1972.

Bicknell, Eugene P. "A Review of the Summer Birds of a Part of the Catskill Mountains." *Transactions of the Linnaean Society of New York* 1 (1882): 113-168.

_____. "A Sketch of the Home of Hylocichla Aliciae Bicknelli, Ridgway, With Some Critical Remarks on the Allies of this New Race." *Bulletin of the Nuttall Ornithological Club* 7, no. 3 (1882): 152-159.

Bierhorst, John. *The Ashokan Catskills: A Natural History.* Fleischmanns, New York: Purple Mountain Press, 1995.

Big Indian-Beaverkill Range Wilderness Area Unit Management Plan. New Paltz, New York: New York State Department of Environmental Conservation, June 1993.

Bogardus, Mary. *Crisis in the Catskills.* New York: Vantage Press, 1960.

Brandt, Clare. *An American Aristocracy: The Livingstons.* Garden City, New York: Doubleday, 1986.

Brass Buttons and Leather Boots. Sullivan County Historical Society, 1963.

Brent, William T. "Wild Pigeons." In *Picturesque Ulster*, edited by Richard Lionel De Lisser. Kingston, New York: Styles and Bruyn Publishing, 1896-1905: 164-165, reprinted Cornwallville, New York: Hope Farm Press, 1968.

Brooks, Doris West. *The Old Eagle-Nester, The Lost Legends of the Catskills*. Hensonville, New York: Black Dome Press, 1992.

Brooks, Karl F. *A Catskill Flora and Economic Botany*. 5 vols. Albany, New York: New York State Museum, 1979-1984.

Bruegel, Martin. *Farm, Shop, Landing: The Rise of a Market Society in the Hudson Valley, 1780-1860*. Durham: Duke University Press, 2002.

Burgin, Bryan E. "The Catskill Deer Park." *The Conservationist*, April-May 1973, 11, 44.

Burroughs, John. "The Apple." In *Picturesque Catskills, Greene County*, edited by Richard Lionel De Lisser. Northampton, Massachusetts: Picturesque Publishing Company, 1894, reprinted Cornwallville, New York: Hope Farm Press, 1967.

_____. *The Heart of Burroughs's Journals*. Clara Barrus, ed. Port Washington, New York: Kennikat Press, 1967. Originally published New York: Houghton Mifflin, 1928.

_____. *John Burroughs Talks: His Reminiscences and Comments*. Clifton Johnson, ed. New York: Houghton Mifflin, 1922.

_____. Letters to Myron Benton. 14 January 1893, 6 November 1893. Berg Collection, New York Public Library.

_____. *The Life and Letters of John Burroughs*. Clara Barrus, ed. 2 vols. New York: Russell and Russell, 1968. Originally published New York: Houghton Mifflin, 1925.

_____. *My Boyhood*. Garden City, New York: Doubleday, Page and Company, 1922.

_____. *The Writings of John Burroughs*. Riverby Edition, 23 vols. New York: Houghton Mifflin, 1904-1923.

Burroughs, John and Ludella Peck. *John Burroughs and Ludella Peck*. New York: Harold Vinal, 1925.

Bussy, Ethel H. *Margaretville: History and Stories of Margaretville and the Surrounding Area*. Privately printed, 1960.

Butterfield, L. H., ed. *Adams Family Correspondence*. Vol. 2. The Adams Papers. Cambridge, Massachusetts: Harvard University Press, 1963.

Butterfield, Roger. *The American Past: A History of the United States From Concord to the Nuclear Age*. New York: Simon and Schuster, 1957.

Buttrick, R. L. "Woodstock's Woods and Their Effect On Its History and People." *Publications of the Woodstock Historical Society* 11 (1933): 12-21.

Carpenter, Charles F. "The Catskill Preserve." In *Second Annual Report of the Forest Commission of the State of New York*. Albany, New York, 1887, 115-116.

Case, Daniel. "The Ultimate Thrush." *Kaaterskill Life* 16, no. 2 (Summer 2001): 32-34.

The Catskill Mountains, The Most Picturesque Mountain Region on the Globe. Kingston, New York: Freeman Publishing Company, 1894, reprinted, 1916.

Catskill Park State Land Master Plan, Draft Revision. Albany, New York: New York State Department of Environmental Conservation, August 2003.

The Catskills, An Illustrated Hand-Book and Souvenir. Kingston, New York: Ferris Publication Company, 1897.

Catskill Trails. Albany, New York: State of New York Conservation Department, 1969.

Cazden, Norman, Herbert Haufrecht, and Norman Studer, eds. *Folk Songs of the Catskills.* Albany, New York: State University of New York Press, 1982.

Chase, Sherret S. "The Catskills of New York, Past, Present and Potential." *American Forests,* August 1967, 46.

Child, Hamilton. *Gazetteer and Business Directory of Sullivan County, N. Y. For 1872-3.* Syracuse, New York: The Journal Office, 1872.

Christman, Henry. *Tin Horns and Calico.* New York: Henry Holt, 1945, reprinted Cornwallville, New York: Hope Farm Press, 1978.

Clearwater, Alphonso T., ed. *The History of Ulster County, New York.* Kingston, New York: W. J. Van Deusen, 1907.

Clemens, Samuel L. *A Connecticut Yankee In King Arthur's Court.* New York: Harper and Row, 1889.

Colvin, Verplanck. In *24th Annual Report on the New York State Museum of Natural History.* Albany, New York, 1870.

Commager, Henry Steele, ed. *The Era of Reform, 1830-1860.* New York: D. Van Nostrand, 1960.

Commemorative Biographical Record of Ulster County, New York. Chicago: J. H. Beers, 1896.

Conway, John. *Retrospect: An Anecdotal History of Sullivan County, New York.* Fleischmanns, New York: Purple Mountain Press, 1996.

_____. "View From Slide Mountain Attracted Tourists." *Times Herald-Record,* 16 February 1994, 6.

Cook, John C. "From Farmland to Forest." *The Conservationist,* October-November 1974, 10-13.

Cooper, James Fenimore. *The Pioneers.* New York: New American Library, 1964.

Cornish, J. Marion, Rev. "Reminiscences of Pine Hill." Published in installments, Pine Hill *Sentinel,* 1906.

Crevecoeur, J. Hector St. John. *Letters from an American Farmer.* New York: E. P. Dutton, 1957. First published, 1782.

Cronon, William. *Changes in the Land: Indians, Colonists, and the Ecology of New England.* New York: Hill and Wang, 1983.

Crosby, Maunsell Schieffelin. "In Memoriam: Eugene Pintard Bicknell, 1859-1925." *The Auk: A Quarterly Journal of Ornithology* 43, no. 2 (April 1926): 143-149.

Cuyler, Theodore L. "The Heart of the Catskills." First published in the New York *Evangelist.* Reprinted in the promotional booklet *The New Grand Hotel, Catskill Mountains,* edited by Edward A. Gillett, 1887.

_____. "A Sabbath On the Catskills." In *The Catskill Mountains and the Region Around,* edited by Charles Rockwell. New York: Taintor Brothers, 1867, 259-262, reprinted Cornwallville, New York: Hope Farm Press, 1973.

C. W. V. "On Top Of The Catskills." The *Argus,* 1 September 1875.

Daley, Mary Wood. "Birds of Frost Valley, Slide Mountain Region, Southern Catskills." *The Auk* 39, no. 2 (April 1922): 176-188.

Dangerfield, George. *Chancellor Robert R. Livingston of New York, 1746-1813.* New York: Harcourt, Brace, 1960.

Davidson, Howard Fletcher. *Delaware County: Fur Trading to Farming.* Delhi, New York: R. B. Decker Advertising, 1976.

Davis, De Witt C. "Town of Olive." In *The History of Ulster County, New York,* edited by Alphonso T. Clearwater. Kingston, New York: W. J. Van Deusen, 1907: 324-331.

Davis, Elwyn C. Interviews by author. September 1973-January 1975.

_____. *West Shokan: The Eden of the Catskills.* West Shokan, New York: Ladies' Aid Society of the Olive-Shokan Baptist Church, 1930.

Day, Gordon. "The Indian as an Ecological Factor in the Northeastern Forest." *Ecology* 34, no. 2: 329-346.

De Lisser, Richard Lionel, ed. *Picturesque Catskills, Greene County.* Northampton, Massachusetts: Picturesque Publishing Company, 1894, reprinted Cornwallville, New York: Hope Farm Press, 1967.

_____. *Picturesque Ulster.* Kingston, New York: Styles and Bruyn Publishing Company, 1896-1905, reprinted Cornwallville, New York: Hope Farm Press, 1968.

De Natale, Douglas. *Two Stones for Every Dirt: The Story of Delaware County, New York.* Fleischmanns, New York: Purple Mountain Press, 1987.

Denman, Carol M. *Denman Family Cookbook.* Privately printed, 1995.

Denman, Paul and James Cooper. Interviews by author. 16 October 2000, 4 June 2001, 9 June 2001.

Denning, William H. Letter to Richard D. Childs of Grahamsville, New York, Sullivan County. 6 April 1841. Xeroxed copy in author's collection.

Dwight, Henry E. "Account of the Catskill Mountains." *American Journal of Science and Arts* 2, no. 1 (1820): 11-29.

Dwight, Timothy. *Travels in New-England and New-York.* Barbara Miller Solomon, ed. Cambridge, Massachusetts: Belknap Press of Harvard University, 1969. First published, 1821-22, 4 vols.

Eckert, Allan W. *The Silent Sky: The Incredible Extinction of the Passenger Pigeon.* Dayton, Ohio: Landfall Press, 1965.

Edwards, William. *Memoirs of Colonel William Edwards.* Washington, D. C.: Privately printed, 1897.

Ellis, David Maldwyn and others. *A History of New York State.* Ithaca, New York: Cornell University Press, revised edition, 1967.

_____. *Landlords and Farmers in the Hudson-Mohawk Region, 1790-1850.* Ithaca, New York: Cornell University Press, 1946, reprinted New York: Octagon Books, 1967.

_____. "The Yankee Invasion of New York, 1783-1850." *New York History* 32 (January 1951): 3-17.

Erts, George. "Denning History." Unpublished ms. in typescript, 25 February 1975.

Evers, Alf. *The Catskills: From Wilderness to Woodstock.* Garden City, New York: Doubleday, 1972.

_____. *In Catskill Country.* Woodstock, New York: Overlook Press, 1995.

_____. Interview by author. 18 August 1997.

_____. "The Shandaken Mountains and Asher Durand." *Ulster County Townsman*, 5 January 1961, 2.

_____. "Slide Mountain—King of the Catskills." *The Conservationist*, June-July 1961, 2-6, 34.

_____. "The Tannery Brook." *Woodstock Times*, 10 April 1975, 13.

Faris, John T. *Roaming the Eastern Mountains*. New York: Farrar and Rinehart, 1932.

Faulkner, Harold U. and Mark Starr. *Labor in America*. New York: Harper and Brothers, 1944.

Fischer, David H. *Albion's Seed: Four British Folkways in America*. New York: Oxford University Press, 1989.

Forbes, John. *The Physician's Holiday, or a Month in Switzerland in the Summer of 1848*. London, 1853.

Forbush, Edward Howe, contributing editor and others. *Birds of America*. 3 Parts. Garden City, New York: Garden City Publishing Company, 1936.

Fowler, Barnett. "Water for Gotham: The Reservoirs of New York City—Built, Building, and To Be Built." *The Conservationist*, August-September 1948, 14-15.

Fox, Dixon Ryan. *Yankees and Yorkers*. New York: University Press, 1940.

Fox, William F. "History of the Lumber Industry in the State of New York." In *Sixth Annual Report of the Forest, Fish and Game Commission of the State of New York, 1900*. Albany, New York, 1901, 237-305.

Francis, Austin M. *Catskill Rivers, Birthplace of American Fly Fishing*. Piscataway, New Jersey: Winchester, 1983.

Freeman, Ruth. *The Frugal Housewife*. Watkins Glen, New York: Century House, 1957.

French, J. H. *Gazetteer of the State of New York*: R. Pearsall Smith, 1860.

Frome, Michael. *Strangers in High Place: The Story of the Great Smoky Mountains*. Garden City, New York: Doubleday, 1966.

Gale, Lonnie and Ruth. *Shandaken, New York: A Pictorial History*. Fleischmanns, New York: Purple Mountain Press, 1999.

Galusha, Diane. *Liquid Assets: A History of New York City's Water System*. Fleischmanns, New York: Purple Mountain Press, 1999.

Gardiner, Lawrence. "Prattsville's Master Tanner." *The Catskills* 2, no. 2 (Spring 1974): 4-10.

Gates, Paul W. *The Farmer's Age: Agriculture, 1815-1860*. 2nd ed. New York: Harper and Row, 1968.

Gerow, Joshua. *Alder Lake, A Symposium of Nostalgic and Natural Observations*. Liberty, New York: Fuelane Press, 1953.

Gillett, Edward A., ed. *The New Grand Hotel, Catskill Mountains*. Promotional booklets, 1887 and 1888.

Giuliano, Gina. "Eight Generations: The Eckert Family in West Shokan, 1792-1999." *Kaatskill Life* 14, no. 4 (Winter 1999-2000): 16-23.

Gold, David M., ed. *The River and the Mountains: Readings in Sullivan County History*. South Fallsburg, New York: Marielle, 1994.

Gould, Jay. *History of Delaware County and the Border Wars of New York*. Roxbury, New York: Keeny and Gould, 1856.

Greeley, Horace. *New-York Weekly Tribune*, 18 April 1843, 102.

Griffeth, Henry. "The Town of Shandaken." In *The History of Ulster County, New York*, edited by Alphonso T. Clearwater. Kingston, New York: W. J. Van Deusen, 1907: 366-372.

Guyot, Arnold Henry. *The Earth and Man: Lectures on Comparative Physical Geography, in its Relation to the History of Mankind*. C. C. Felton, trans. Boston: Gould and Lincoln, 4th ed., revised, 1851. First published, 1849.

_____. *Map of the Catskill Mountains*. New York: Scribners, 1879, 1880.

_____. "On the Appalachian Mountain System." *American Journal of Science and Arts* [Second Series] 31, no. 92 (March 1861): 157-187.

_____. "On the Physical Structure and Hypsometry of the Catskill Mountain Region." *American Journal of Science* [Third Series] 19, no. 114 (June 1880): 429-451.

Haring, H. A. *Our Catskill Mountains*. New York: G. P. Putnam's, 1931.

Hasbrouck, Kenneth E. "History of the Town of Denning." In *The History of Ulster County With Emphasis Upon the Last 100 Years*. Ulster County Historical Society, 1984.

Hawke, David Freeman. *Everyday Life In Early America*. New York: Harper and Row, 1988.

Haynes, Clara A. "Saga of Highmount." 3 pp. unpublished ms. in typescript, 1949.

Haynes, Lena Knapp. "Pioneers Found Dry Brook to Their Liking." *Catskill Mountain News*, 15 August 1963, 2-3.

Hedrick, Ulysses Prentiss. *A History of Agriculture in the State of New York*. New York: Hill and Wang, 1966. First published, 1933.

_____. *The Land of the Crooked Tree*. New York: Oxford University Press, 1948.

Heilprin, Angelo. "The Catskill Mountains." *Bulletin of the American Geographical Society* 39, no. 4 (1907): 193-201.

Hendricks, Howard. "The Town of Hardenburgh." In *The History of Ulster County, New York*, edited by Alphonso T. Clearwater. Kingston, New York: W. J. Van Deusen, 1907.

Higgins, Ruth L. *Expansion in New York With Especial Reference to the Eighteenth Century*. Columbus, Ohio: Ohio State University Press, 1931.

History of Delaware County, N. Y. New York: W. W. Munsell and Company, 1880.

Hitchcock, Elwood. *Big Hollow*. Hensonville, New York: Black Dome Press, 1993.

Hoffman, A. W. "The Passing of the Hemlock." In *Picturesque Ulster*, edited by Richard Lionel De Lisser. Kingston, New York: Styles and Bruyn Publishing, 1896: 185-191, reprinted Cornwallville, New York: Hope Farm Press, 1968.

Hope, Jack E. "The Catskill Tanning Industry—Its Rise and Fall." *The Conservationist*, October-November 1960, 28-29.

Horne, Field. *The Greene County: A History*. Hensonville, New York: Black Dome Press, 1994.

Huston, Reeve. *Land and Freedom: Rural Society, Popular Protest, and Party Politics in Antebellum New York*. New York: Oxford University Press, 2000.

Ingersoll, Ernest. "At the Gateway of the Catskills." *Harper's New Monthly Magazine* 54 (December 1876-May 1877): 816-824.

Irving, Washington. *A History of New York*. New Haven, Connecticut: College and University Press, 1964.

Jacobson, Alice H. *Beneath Pepacton Waters*. Andes, New York. Privately printed, 1988.

Jacobson, Alice and Robert. *Echoes Along the Delaware*. Andes, New York. Privately printed, 1992.

Kendeigh, Charles S. "Breeding Birds of the Beech-Maple-Hemlock Community." *Ecology* 27, no. 3 (July 1946): 226-245.

Kerr, Randolph and Norman Van Valkenburgh. "Catskill Forest Preserve." *The Conservationist*, April-May 1973, 8-10.

Kierner, Cynthia A. *Traders and Gentlefolk: The Livingstons of New York, 1675-1790*. Ithaca, New York: Cornell University Press, 1992.

Kimball, Henry, "The Catskill Mountains." Kingston *Daily Freeman*, 31 August 1874, reprinted from the *Brooklyn Eagle*.

Klein, Maury. *The Life and Legend of Jay Gould*. Baltimore: Johns Hopkins University Press, 1986.

Kortright, Agnes R. *Old Neversink and Surroundings*. Privately printed, September 1992.

Krout, John Allen and Dixon Ryan Fox. *The Completion of Independence, 1790-1830*. New York: Macmillan, 1944.

Kubik, Dorothy. *A Free Soil—A Free People: The Anti-Rent War in Delaware County, New York*. Fleischmanns, New York: Purple Mountain Press, 1997.
Kudish, Michael. *The Catskill Forest: A History*. Fleischmanns, New York: Purple Mountain Press, 2000.

_____. "Catskill Forest History: Peekamoose From the Rondout." *Adirondac* 49, no. 4 (May 1985): 17-18.

_____. "First Growth in the Catskills." *Adirondac* 60, no. 4 (July-August 1996): 18-20.

_____. "Forest History of Frost Valley." *Adirondac* 49 no. 3 (April 1985): 16-18.

_____. Public lectures. Belleayre Mountain Ski Center. 9 June 1996, 7 June 1998, 29 August 1999. Catskill Center. 11 June 2000.

_____. "Vegetational History of the Catskill High Peaks." Ph.D. diss., State University College of Forestry at Syracuse University, 1971.

Lane, Helen, ed. *The Story of Walton*. Walton, New York: Walton Historical Society, 1975.

Link, Arthur S. *The American People: A History*. Vol. 1. Arlington, Illinois: AHM Publishing Corporation, 1981.

List of Lands in the Forest Preserve. Albany, New York: New York State Forest, Fish and Game Commission, 1905.

Livingston, R. R. Letter to R. Livingston. 4 June 1776. Franklin Delano Roosevelt Library, Hyde Park, New York.

"Local News." Pine Hill *Sentinel*, 13 July 1887.

Longstreth, T. Morris. *The Catskills*. New York: Century, 1918.

Majewski, John, Christopher Baer, and Daniel B. Klein. "Responding to Relative Discipline: The Plank Road Boom of Antebellum New York." *The Journal of*

Economic History 52, no. 1 (March 1993): 106-122.

Marranca, Bonnie, ed. *A Hudson Valley Reader*. Woodstock, New York: Overlook Press, 1991.

Mather, J. H. *Geography of New York*. New York, 1847.

McIntosh, Robert P. "The Forest Cover of the Catskill Mountain Region, New York, as Indicated in Land Survey Records." *The American Midland Naturalist* 68, no. 2 (October 1962): 409-423.

_____. *The Forests of the Catskill Mountains, New York*. Cornwallville, New York: Hope Farm Press, 1977. Previously published, *Ecological Monographs* 42 (Spring 1972): 143-161.

McIntosh, Robert P. and R. T. Hurley. "The Spruce-Fir Forests of the Catskill Mountains." *Ecology* 45 (Spring 1964): 314-326.

McMartin, Barbara. *Hides, Hemlocks and Adirondack History: How the Tanning Industry Influenced the Region's Growth*. Utica, New York: North Country Books, 1992.

Medsger, Oliver. "Two Months in the Southern Catskills." *Memoirs of the Torrey Botanical Club* 17 (1918): 294-300.

Meinig, D. W. "Geography of Expansion, 1785-1855." In *Geography of New York State*, edited by John H. Thompson. Syracuse, New York: Syracuse University Press, 1966.

Mershorn, W. B. *The Passenger Pigeon*. Deposit, New York: The Outing Press, 1907.

Millen, Patricia. *Bare Trees: Zadock Pratt, Master Tanner and the Story of What Happened to the Catskill Mountain Forests*. Hensonville, New York: Black Dome Press, 1995.

Miller, Alfred W. *Fishless Days, Angling Nights*. New York: Crown, 1971.

Miller, Myrtle Hardenbergh. *The Hardenbergh Family: A Genealogical Compilation*. New York: The American Historical Company, 1958.

Monroe, John D. *Chapters in the History of Delaware County, New York*. Delhi, New York: Delaware County Historical Association, 1949.

Morgan, Ted. *Wilderness at Dawn: The Settling of the North American Continent*. New York: Simon and Shuster, 1993.

Muise, Jeff. *Old Bob's Gift: Life in the Catskill Mountains of the 1850s*. Wappingers Falls, New York: Shawangunk Press, 1996.

Mushkat, Jerome and Joseph G. Rayback. *Martin Van Buren: Law, Politics, and the Shaping of Republican Ideology*. DeKalb, Illinois: Northern Illinois University Press, 1997.

Nevins, Allan, ed. *American Social History as Recorded by British Travellers*. New York, 1923.

Norcross, Frank. *A History of the New York Swamp*. New York: Chiswick Press, 1901.

Nye, Russel Blaine. *The Cultural Life of the New Nation, 1776-1830*. New York: Harper and Row, 1960.

Ogburn, Charlton. "The Passing of the Passenger Pigeon." *American Heritage* 12 (June 1961): 30-33, 90-91.

_____. *The Southern Appalachians: A Wilderness Quest*. New York: William Morrow, 1975.

Overbaugh, Dewitt Clinton. *The Hermit of the Catskills*. New York: G. W. Dillingham, 1900.

Owen, George W. *The Leach Club; or the Mysteries of the Catskills*. Boston: Lee and Shephard, 1874.

Partridge, Michael. *Early Agricultural Machinery*. New York: Praeger, 1969.
_____. *Farm Tools Through the Ages*. New York: Graphic Society, 1974.

Petrides, George A. *Trees and Shrubs*. Boston: Houghton Mifflin, 1956.

Phillips, Sandra and Linda Weintraub, eds. *Charmed Places*. New York: Harry N. Abrams, 1988.

Pine Hill *Sentinel*, 1 December 1886, 22 June 1887, 13 July 1887.

Podskoch, Martin. *Fire Towers of the Catskills: Their History and Lore*. Fleischmanns, New York: Purple Mountain Press, 2000.

Pokagon (Chief). *Chautauguan* 22, no. 20 (November 1895).

Powell, Joan and Irene Barnhart. *Beaverkill Valley, A Journey Through Time*. Lew Beach, New York: B. P. Publishing Company, 1999.

Pratt, Zadock. *Chronological Biography of the Honorable Zadock Pratt of Prattsville, N.Y.* New York: Shoe and Leather Press, 1862, reprinted, 1868.

Prout, Henry Hedges. *Old Times in Windham*. Originally published in *The Windham Journal*, 18 February 1869-31 March 1870, reprinted Cornwallville, New York: Hope Farm Press, 1970.

Purcell, Barbara Wakefield, ed. *Time and the Valley: Story of the Upper Rondout Valley*. Town of Neversink Bicentennial Commission, 1978.

Quinlan, James E. *History of Sullivan County*. Liberty, New York: G. M. Beebe and W. T. Morgans, 1873, reprinted South Fallsburg, New York: Fallsburg Printing Company, 1965.

Randall, Doris Dutcher. Interview by the author. 1 March 2005.

Recknagel, A. B. "The Forests of the Catskills." *The Conservationist*, December 1920, 179-182.

Renehan, Edward J. *John Burroughs: An American Naturalist*. Post Mills, Vermont: Chelsea Green, 1992, reprinted Hensonville, New York: Black Dome Press, 1998.

Report of the Forestry Commission of the State of New York. Albany, New York, 1886.

Resorts of the Catskills. The Architectural League of New York. New York: St. Martin's Press, 1979.

Reynolds, George B. *Memories of Long Ago*. Published in *Republican Watchman*, Monticello, New York and *Ellenville Press*, Ellenville, New York, 1936, reprinted as booklet, n. d.

Rhoads, William B. *Kingston, New York: The Architectural Guide*. Hensonville, New York: Black Dome Press, 2003.

Ridgway, Robert. "Descriptions of Two New Thrushes From the United States." *Proceedings of the United States National Museum* 4 (1882): 374-379.

Rockwell, Charles. *The Catskill Mountains and the Region Around*. New York: Taintor Brothers, 1867, reprinted Cornwallville, New York: Hope Farm Press, 1973.

Rotenstein, David S. "Tanbark Tycoons: Palen Family Sullivan County Tanneries, 1832-1871." *The Hudson Valley Regional Review* 15, no. 2 (September 1998): 1-42.

Shafer, Jamie O. "A Propper Yankee in Central New York: The Diary of Mary Bishop Cushman, 1795-1797." *New York History* 79, no. 3 (July 1998): 255-312.

Shultz, Herbert L. *A Winnisook Chronicle, 1886-1986.* Privately printed, 1986.

Sickler, Vera Van Steenbergh. *History of the Town of Olive, 1823-1973.* Privately printed, 1973.

Sixth Annual Report of the Forest, Fish and Game Commission of the State of New York. Albany, New York, 1901.

Slide Mountain Wilderness Unit Management Plan. New Paltz, New York: New York State Department of Environmental Conservation, October 1998.

Smith, Nancy T., ed. *And They Stayed...Hotels & Boarding Houses in the Town of Shandaken.* Privately printed, 2007.

Smith, Page. *The Rise of Industrial America: A People's History of the Post-Reconstruction Era.* Vol. 6. New York: McGraw-Hill, 1984.

Steadman, David W. "And Live on Pigeon Pie." *The Conservationist,* April 1996, 20-23.

Stephens, Ann S. "The Tanner and the Hemlock." *New York Illustrated News,* reprinted in *The Prattsville Advocate,* 2 June 1853.

Steuding, Bob. *A Catskill Mountain Journal.* Fleischmanns, New York: Purple Mountain Press, 1990.

_____. *The Last of the Handmade Dams: The Story of the Ashokan Reservoir.* Fleischmanns, New York: Purple Mountain Press, 1985.

_____. *Rondout: A Hudson River Port.* Fleischmanns, New York: Purple Mountain Press, 1995.

Stone, Irving. *They Also Ran.* New York: New American Library, 1968. First published, 1943.

Stout, N.J. "Catskill Wilderness Areas." In *Tenth Annual Report of the Joint Legislative Committee on Natural Resources.* Legislative document 41. Albany, New York: State of New York, 1961.

Struik, Dirk T. *Yankee Science in the Making.* New York: Collier Books, 1962 ed.

Studer, Norman. *A Catskill Woodsman: Mike Todd's Story.* Fleischmanns, New York: Purple Mountain Press, 1988.

_____. "Folklore From A Valley That Died." *New York Folklore Quarterly* 12, no. 3 (Autumn 1956): 192-199.

Sundown Wild Forest Unit Management Plan. New Paltz, New York: New York State Department of Environmental Conservation, April 1996.

Sutherland, Daniel E. *The Expansion of Everyday Life, 1860-1876.* New York: Harper and Row, 1989.

Sweet, A. T. and Wilber Secor. *Soil Survey of Ulster County, New York.* Washington, D.C.: United States Department of Agriculture. Series 1934, no. 22, June 1940.

Sylvester, Nathaniel Bartlett. *History of Ulster County, New York.* Philadelphia: Everts and Peck, 1880.

Teale, Edwin Way. *North With the Spring.* New York: Dodd, Mead and Company, 1951.

Thaler, Jerome. *Catskill Weather.* Fleischmanns, New York: Purple Mountain Press, 1996.

Thompson, John H., ed. *Geography of New York State*. Syracuse, New York: Syracuse University Press, 1966.

Thoreau, Henry David. "Ktaadn." *The Maine Woods*. In *Henry David Thoreau*. New York: The Library of America, 1985.

_____. *The Portable Thoreau*. Carl Bode, ed. New York: Viking Penguin, 1982 ed.

Tiffany, Lena O. B. *Pioneers of the Beaverkill Valley*. Laurens, New York: Village Printer, 1976.

Tindall, George B. and David E. Shi. *America: A Narrative History*. New York: Norton, 1999.

Titus, Robert. *The Catskills: A Geological Guide*. Fleischmanns, New York: Purple Mountain Press, 1993.

_____. *The Catskills In The Ice Age*. Fleischmanns, New York: Purple Mountain Press, 1996.

Tornes, Lawrence A. *Soil Survey of Ulster County, New York*. Washington, D. C.: United States Department of Agriculture, 1979.

Town of Shandaken. Shandaken, New York: Town of Shandaken Bicentennial Commission, 1976.

Trimm, Lee S. "The Bark Peelers." *The Conservationist*, August-September 1958, 28-29.

Trippe, Martin T. "Birds Found Breeding in the Catskill Mountains." *American Naturalist* 6 (1872): 47-48.

Turner, Benjamin. "Olive History Given by Turner." Mimeographed copy of address given at West Shokan, New York, 4 July 1876.

Van Cleef, J. S. "Recollections of 'Old Times'." *Forest and Stream*, 20 May 1899.

Van Every, Dale. *The Ark of Empire: The American Frontier, 1784-1803*. New York: William Morrow, 1963.

Van Loan, Walton. "Pine Hill As A Summer Resort." Pine Hill *Sentinel*, 22 June 1887.

Van Loan's Catskill Mountain Guide. New York: Dudley Press, 1914.

Van Put, Ed. *The Beaverkill*. New York: Lyons and Burford, 1996.

Van Valkenburgh, Norman J. *The Forest Preserve of New York State in the Adirondack and Catskill Mountains: A Short History*. Fleischmanns, New York: Purple Mountain Press, 1996.

_____. "History of the Catskill Park and Forest Preserve." In *The Catskill Park: Inside the Blue Line*, edited by Norman J. Van Valkenburgh and Christopher W. Olney. Hensonville, New York: Black Dome Press, 2004.

_____. *Land Acquisition for New York State: An Historical Perspective*. Arkville, New York: Catskill Center, 1985.

Van Wagenen, Jared. *The Golden Age of Homespun*. Ithaca, New York: Cornell University Press, 1953.

Van Zandt, Roland. *The Catskill Mountain House*. New Brunswick, New Jersey: Rutgers University Press, 1966, reprinted Hensonville, New York: Black Dome Press, 1991.

Waddell, Ted. "Denmans Celebrate 200 Years in Neversink Valley." *Sullivan County Democrat*, August 1995.

Wermuth, Thomas S. "Economic Opportunity and Moral Economy in the Hudson Valley During the American Revolution." *The Hudson Valley Regional Review* 14, no. 2 (September 1997): 5-23.

_____. *Rip Van Winkle's Neighbors: The Transformation of Rural Society in the Hudson Valley, 1720-1850.* Albany, New York: State University of New York Press, 2001.

West, Edward G. "The Catkills: 'Here the Works of Man Dwindle'." *The Conservationist*, October-November 1962, 6-8.

Westbrook, Perry D. *John Burroughs.* New York: Twayne, 1974.

_____. "John Burroughs and the Transcendentalists." *Emerson Society Quarterly* No. 55, Part 2 (Second Quarter 1969): 47-55.

Wiles, Richard. "The Tanning Industry in Greene County." *Hudson Valley Studies* (June 1983): 8-14.

_____. *Windham.* Saugerties, New York: Hope Farm Press, 1985.

Willis, Joseph F. "Forest-Based Industries." In *The River and the Mountains: Readings in Sullivan County History*, edited by David M. Gold. South Fallsburg, New York: Marielle Press, 1994: 154-162.

Wiltse, Leah Showers. *Pioneer Days in the Catskill High Peaks.* Shirley Wiltse Dunn, ed. Hensonville, New York: Black Dome Press, 1999.

Wingate, Charles F. "Climbing the Catskills." *Country Life in America* 3 (June 1905): 219-220.

Wright, Monroe H. *Along the Neversink in the Seventies.* Liberty, New York: The Liberty Register, n.d.

Zimm, Louise Hasbrouck and others. *Southeastern New York.* 3 vols. New York: Lewis Historical, 1946.

ACKNOWLEDGMENTS

FEW BOOKS OF THIS SORT are written without help. Undoubtedly, this history has benefited from the generosity of many people. Liberally and open-handedly, these good folks have assisted the author, during the many years in which this book has been researched and written. Admittedly, the list which follows is a long one. Thus, with the hope that I shall be forgiven, if I have forgotten anyone through oversight, I gratefully acknowledge my gratitude to: Annon Adams, Barbara Adams, Gary Alexander, George Allen, Jim Andrews, Anita and Spider Barbour, Irene Barnhart, Raymond Beecher, James Behrens, Evelyn Bennett, Joel Bernstein, Jack Bierhorst, Nancy Boulin, David Bronson, Bob Brown, Eve Fairbairn Budd, Jim Burggraf, Bruce Burgher, Ollie Burgher, Rosalie and Bob Burgher, Frank Carle, Patricia Carroll-Mathes, Ralph and Lois Caterino, Helen Chase, Sherret Chase, Don Christiana, Gail Christiancy, John Conway, Jim Cooper, Brendan Coyne, Janet Crawshaw, Virgil Curtis, Herb Cutler, Bill and Tildy Davenport, Whitt Davenport, Amy Davis, Elwyn Davis, Mrs. Ferris Davis, Phil Davis, Bruce Denman, Lee Denman, Paul and Carol Denman, Anne Donovan, Rowland Dutcher, Buddy Eckert, Karlyn Elia, Cloyd and Martha Belle Elias, Alf Evers, Sally Fairbairn, Mark and Kayla Feldman, Brian and Jackie Fennelly, Ed Ford, Lonnie Gale, Ed Garbe, Lew Gardner, Fred Gerty, Bill Golden, Ethel Gray, Joan Voss Greenwood, John Greklek, Roy Gumpel, Phil and Marie Halzell, John Ham, Maria Harding, Herb Haufrecht, Edwina Henderson, George Hendricks, Bob Hill, Justine and Hillard Hommel, Jeremiah Horrigan, Maurice Hungiville, Louise Hunter, Dexter Jeannotte, Hugh and Wally John, Bob Johnson, Amanda Jones, Eric Kalleberg, Rich Katims, Joe Keefe, Elizabeth Burroughs Kelley, Hugh Kelly, Ester Kelsey, Jeannie Kerr, Les Kiersted, John Kokas, Doug Koop, Mike Kudish, Art Kurtznacker, Woody Landers, Bonnie Langston, Mike LeFevre, Pat Legg, Bert Leifeld, Joan Studer Levine, Chet Lyons, Mac MacCreery, Al Marks, Jim Matthews, Harlowe McClain, Tom McGrath, Marilyn McHugh, Jim McTague, Haig Meshejian, Jim Mikesh, Paul Miller, Tom Miner, Ralph Moseley, Jeff Muise, Ernest Myer, Bill Nelson, Jerry Novesky, Ed Ocker, Bob O'Harrow, Dick Olsen, Seward Osborne, Lisa Phillips, Charles Platt, Tim Potts, Joan Powell, Mrs. William Powers, Steve Preston, George Profous, Frank Rafferty, Doris Dutcher Randall, Barbara Shultz Redfield, Kent Reeves, Jay Rifenbary, Ron and Shirley Rifenburg, Hobart Rowe, Bill and Pat Rudge, David Rylance, Barry Samuels, William Sarles, Thelma Schwab, Blaise Schweitzer, Nelson Sears, Nelson Shultis, Dick Shults, Herb Shultz, Ethel Shurter, Dan Shuster, Peter Sinclair, Agnes Scott Smith, Jane Smith, Jean Smith, Mabel Parker Smith, Nancy Smith, Frederic Snyder, Jackie Steuding Soltis, Bill Spangenberger, Willard Squier, Hilarie Staton, Dale Stein, Bob Stewart, Terry Tedeschi, Ed and Lulu Thiel, John Tisch, Bob Titus, Gene Turgeon, Kevin Umhey, Fernando Valdivia, George Van Sickle, Norm Van Valkenburgh, Roland Van Zandt, Roger Vogt, John Wadlin, Beth Waterman, Mabel Weidner, Naiomi Weiss, Ed West, John White, Arthur Wicks, Roger and Chris Winne, Ray Wood, and Pat Yonta.

In addition, I wish to thank the following individuals and the archives, libraries, organizations, and institutions in which they serve: Larry Berk and Kari Mack and the staff of the MacDonald DeWitt Library at Ulster County Community College, especially Roberta Walsh, Curator of the Local History Collection, and Joyce Carey, Melinda Birzenieks, and Bill Russell of Interlibrary Loan; Sylvia Rozzelle at the Town of Olive Archives; the Ulster County Archives; Florence Prehn at the Ulster County Genealogical Society Archives; Ruth Anne Muller and the staff of the Olive Free Library and its Local History Collection; Marion Ryan of the Haviland-Heidgerd Historical Collection at the Elting Memorial Library; Niel Larson of the Hudson Valley Studies Center; the staff at the State University of New York College at New Paltz Sojourner Truth Library; the Library of the New York Historical Association in Cooperstown; the State Library in Albany; the Albany Institute of History and Art; the Berg Collection at the New York Public Library; the Adriance Memorial Library; the Bard and Vassar College Libraries; the Franklin Delano Roosevelt Library; the Vedder Research Library of the Greene County Historical Society; Rich Goring at the Senate House Museum and Library; the New-York Historical Society Library; Joann Gallagher at the Daniel Pierce Library in Grahamsville; Diane DeChillo at the Ellenville Public Library; the Hurley Library; the Kingston Area Library and Local History Room; Charlis Weiss and Alan Bernstein at the Morton Memorial Library in Pine Hill; the Phoenicia Library; the Stone Ridge Library; the West Hurley Public Library; and the Woodstock Public Library.

Also, the Bevier House Museum of the Ulster County Historical Society; D & H Canal Museum; Empire State Railway Museum; Hudson River Maritime Center; Kingston Urban Cultural Park Museum; Klyne Esopus Historical Society Museum; Mountain Top Historical Society; Olive Historical Society; and the Zadock Pratt Museum.

I am, also, deeply grateful to Richard Frisbee for permission to use photographs previously published by Hope Farm Press; to my exceptional publishers Wray and Loni Rominger—this is our fourth book; my colleagues at Ulster County Community College, and President Donald C. Katt and the Board of Trustees, who have consistently and steadfastly supported my work; my able son Miles, who took the author's photograph; my beautiful and accomplished wife Martha, my editor and muse, whose own work with people with disabilities touches and inspires me; and finally, Monica Kiersted Leonardo, longtime friend and ally in historical adventure, without whom these books could not have been written. This book is hers.

INDEX

PURPLE MOUNTAIN PRESS, established in 1973, publishes books of colonial history and books about New York State. Under its Harbor Hill imprint, it also publishes maritime books and distributes the maritime books of Carmania Press (London).

For a free catalog, write Purple Mountain Press, PO Box 309, Fleischmanns, NY 12430-0309, or call 800-325-2665, or fax 845-254-4476, or email purple@catskill.net. On the web at www.catskill.net/purple.